1953

What A Year To Be Born!

Written by
Robin Bennett-Freebairn and Joe Toussaint

Published by Emersive
www.whatayeartobeborn.com

 First published in Great Britain in 2023 by Emersive Limited. The publishers and authors have done their best to ensure the accuracy of all the information in this book. However, they cannot accept responsibility for any consequences arising from the use of this book. ISBN 978-1-73-973543-2.

What happened in 1953? We have a special affinity for the year we were born, but how much do we really know about it? This guide takes you through the highs and lows of an historic year in the midst of the baby boom generation. The colour-coded chapters unlock a wealth of information that brings you closer to what life was like in this milestone year.

Contents

Introduction

1953 was a significant year in British history, marked by several notable events that shaped the country's social, cultural and political landscape. The most significant of these was the Coronation of Queen Elizabeth II. On June 2nd, she was crowned at Westminster Abbey in a ceremony that was watched by millions of people around the world. The coronation marked the beginning of a new Elizabethan era in British history, as the young queen took the throne after the death of her father, King George VI.

June 2nd also saw the announcement of the conquest of Everest. New Zealander Edmund Hillary and Nepalese Tensing Norgay became the first men to reach the summit of the World's highest peak. The year also saw the end of most food rationing in the UK, which had been in place since just after the beginning of World War II. This was a welcome relief for many Britons, who had grown weary of the restrictions on their diet and the long queues for basic necessities, although rationing of some meats and dairy produce would last until 1954.

Another notable event was the discovery of the structure of DNA by James Watson and Francis Crick. Their work, which built on the research of others, revolutionised the field of genetics and laid the foundation for many scientific advances in the decades to come. On a more sombre note, 1953 was also the year of the North Sea Flood, which caused widespread devastation along the coasts of the UK. the Netherlands and Belgium. More than 2,000 people were killed in the disaster, which was caused by a combination of high tides and a severe storm.

The year saw the end of the Korean War, which had begun three years earlier. British forces had been part of the United Nations contingent that fought against North Korea and China with many British soldiers losing their lives in the conflict. In world politics, 1953 was marked by the death of Soviet leader Joseph Stalin, who had been in power for more than two decades. His passing led to a period of uncertainty and power struggles within the Soviet Union, as his eventual successor, Nikita Khrushchev, worked to consolidate his own authority.

The literary world mourned the passing of the poet Dylan Thomas and celebrated the debuts of two of the greatest plays of the twentieth century, *Waiting for Godot* and *The Crucible*. Popular names for children born this year were: Susan, Linda and Christine, for girls and David, John and Stephen, for boys. In football, Arsenal won their seventh league title and Blackpool won the F.A. Cup in what became known as the "Matthews Cup Final." However the English national team was taught a harsh lesson when they were beaten 6-3 by the "Mighty Magyars" of Hungary on home soil at Wembley.

Headline News

The Daily Headlines

No: 4892

THREE HALFPENCE

First Edition

Saturday, February 28, 1953

JAMES WATSON AND FRANCIS CRICK ANNOUNCE THEY HAVE DISCOVERED 'THE SECRET OF LIFE'. DNA IS DECODED.

The Daily Headlines

THREE HALFPENCE

Fritday, May 29, 1953

No: 4979

First Edition

EDMUND HILLARY AND SHERPA TENZING NORGAY MAKE THE FIRST SUCCESSFUL ASCENT OF MOUNT EVEREST

The Daily Headlines

THREE HALFPENCE

Tuesday, June 2, 1953

No: 4983

First Edition

GOD SAVE OUR GRACIOUS QUEEN. ELIZABETH II CROWNED QUEEN AS MILLIONS CHEER AT CORONATION PARADE

The Daily Headlines

No: 5076

THREE HALFPENCE

First Edition

Saturday, September 12, 1953

THE SOCIAL EVENT OF THE SEASON AS SENATOR JOHN F. KENNEDY AND JACQUELINE BOUVIER MARRY IN NEWPORT, RHODE ISLAND, USA

Jan 3rd	Republican Oliver P. Bolton begins his first term in the U.S. Congress, where his mother Frances P. Bolton is already serving. They thus become the first mother and son to serve simultaneously in Congress.
Jan 5th	A British Airways Vickers VC.1 aircraft hits an approach light and crashes into a building at Nutts Corner Airport near Belfast. Only 8 of the 35 passengers survive.
Jan 6th	In New Zealand, Godfrey Bowen sets a world sheep-shearing record by shearing 456 sheep in nine hours. That's nearly one sheep per minute.
Jan 7th	U.S. President Harry S. Truman announces that his country has developed a hydrogen bomb. It is several times more powerful than the atomic bombs dropped on Hiroshima and Nagasaki less than a decade earlier.
Jan 13th	In what is dubbed the "Doctors' Plot", the Soviet newspaper Pravda publishes an article claiming that many of the most senior physicians in the country are plotting to poison the political and military hierarchy. The story is fiction and most of the alleged conspirators are Jewish.
Jan 14th	Hero of the resistance against Nazism during World War II, Marshal Josip Broz Tito is chosen to be President of Yugoslavia.
Jan 18th	In a marked change of policy, Sinn Féin, Ireland's republican party decides, that it will contest all twelve constituencies in the next UK General Election.
Jan 19th	CBS in America airs "Lucy Goes to the Hospital" an episode of I love Lucy, in which Lucy (Lucille Ball) gives birth to her son. 44 million people tune in, more than watch the inauguration of President Dwight D. Eisenhower.
Jan 20th	President Dwight D. Eisenhower is sworn in as 34th President of the USA.
Jan 22nd	Arthur Miller's *The Crucible* opens on Broadway. The play is an allegory of McCarthyism in the United States.
Jan 28th	Derek Bentley is hanged at Wandsworth Prison for his part in the murder of a police officer. Anti-death penalty protesters gather outside.

Jan 31st A severe storm hits Britain. The MV Princess Victoria sinks. 133 people lose their lives including Ulster politicians Maynard Sinclair and Walter Smiles. 44 people are rescued by other vessels.

Feb 1st A surge following the storm of the previous day hits the North Sea coast of England. 307 people are killed in the counties of Lincolnshire, Norfolk, Suffolk and Essex. The surge goes on to wreak havoc in Belgium and The Netherlands.

Feb 5th Children and many grown-ups jump for joy as sweet rationing ends.

Feb 6th English contralto Kathleen Ferrier, who is terminally ill with cancer, is taken from the Covent Garden Opera House on a stretcher after bravely completing the second night of her run in Gluck's *Orfeo ed Euridice*.

Feb 9th In Scotland, the Fraserburgh lifeboat John and Charles Kennedy, capsizes while on the way to escort fishing vessels into harbour during a storm. Six crew members are lost.

Feb 11th President Dwight D. Eisenhower refuses clemency for Julius and Ethel Rosenburg, a couple sentenced to death for spying for the Soviet union.

Feb 12th A 6.6 magnitude earthquake in the Torud region of Iran kills at least 800 people.

Feb 14th It is Chinese New Year and it is the year of the Water Snake. Those born this year are blessed with being very smart, lively and active. Those born before February 14th fall under the sign of the Water Dragon and are far-sighted and persevering.

Feb 26th US Bishop Fulton J. Sheen, at the end of his weekly show, *Life is Worth Living*, reads the assassination scene from Shakespeare's Julius Caesar, with the names of high-ranking Soviet officials replacing the main characters. He concludes stating "Stalin one day must meet his judgement."

Feb 28th James Watson and Francis Crick publicly claim that they and their team have have discovered the structure of the DNA molecule.

Mar 1st	Soviet leader Joseph Stalin suffers a stoke after an all-night party. He falls into a coma.
Mar 5th	Having never regained consciousness following a stroke, Stalin dies.
Mar 5th	On a cold, misty day at Cheltenham, Knock Hard wins the Gold Cup on his second attempt at odds of 11/2. He is trained by legendary Irish horseman Vincent O'Brien.
Mar 6th	Georgy Malenkov succeeds Joseph Stalin as Premier and First Secretary of the Communist Party of the Soviet Union.
Mar 10th	The very first coins bearing the image of Her Majesty Queen Elizabeth II are struck. Her image on the obverse side of the coin is taken from a portrait by artist Mary Gillick.
Mar 12th	A three-day tornado outbreak begins in parts of the United States. It leaves at least 21 dead and causes millions of dollars' worth of damage.
Mar 12th	Nikita Khrushchev is selected First Secretary of the Soviet Communist Party.
Mar 18th	An earthquake hits Western Turkey killing at least 1,000 people.
Mar 19th	The 25th Academy Awards are held at the RKO Pantages Theatre in Hollywood and the NBC International Theatre in New York. It is the first Oscars ceremony to be televised live. There is a huge upset in the Best Picture category as *High Noon* loses out to *The Greatest Show on Earth*.
Mar 20th	Jimmy Carter leaves his family's peanut farm to start nuclear power school, a six-month course covering nuclear power plant operation at the Union College in Schenectady.
Mar 24th	Queen Mary, the Queen's grandmother and Consort to George V, dies.
Mar 28th	The World Professional Match-Play snooker tournament ends in London. Fred Davis defends the crown he won last year.

Mar 29th — The World Table Tennis Championships reach their conclusion in Bucharest, Romania. The British Men's team return triumphant and lift the Swaythling Cup. The home team lift the Women's trophy.

Apr 7th — Swede Dag Hammarskjöld is elected to the post of United Nations Secretary-General. He replaces Norway's Trygve Lie.

Apr 13th — Ian Fleming's first James Bond novel, *Casino Royale* hits the bookshelves.

Apr 13th — The German football team Dynamo Dresden is founded.

Apr 13th — A new radio series, *Partners in Crime*, based on the works of Agatha Christie is launched on the BBC Home Service. It stars Richard Attenborough and Sheila Sim.

Apr 15th — The Cannes Film Festival opens in the South of France. There is a special award for Walt Disney, while *The Wages of Fear*, directed by Henri-Georges Clouzot, scoops the Grand Prix for best film.

Apr 15th — The North Down by-election, brought about by the death of sitting Ulster Unionist MP Walter Smiles, who died in the sinking of the Princess Victoria, results in the unopposed election of another Unionist candidate, Smiles' daughter Patricia Ford. She becomes the first woman to be elected to a Northern Ireland constituency.

Apr 16th — President Eisenhower delivers his "Chance for Peace" speech. In it he states that arms spending is akin to stealing from the people. These are strong words coming from an ex-military man, who had led the combined Allied Forces during the Second World war.

Apr 20th — Singer Frank Sinatra and arranger Nelson Riddle begin recording sessions together at Capitol Studios. They produce some of the best work of Sinatra's career. In jazz, trumpeter Miles Davis, at the height of his heroin addiction, records his album *Miles Davis Volume 2* at WOR Studios in New York.

Apr 21st — The Battle of Chatkol, part of the Korean War, ends after the Belgium Volunteer Corps for Korea holds its position for 55 consecutive days.

Apr 25th	Brit Francis Crick and American James Watson publish "Molecular Structure of Nucleic Acids: A Structure for Deoxyribose Nucleic Acid", their description of the double helix structure of DNA.
May 2nd	BOAC Flight 783 breaks up in mid-air and crashes near Calcutta, India. All 43 on board are killed.
May 2nd	The F.A. Cup final is held at Wembley in front of a crowd of 100,000. It features a stand-out performance by Stanley Matthews and would become known as the "Matthews Cup Final". Matthew's Blackpool beat Bolton Wanderers 4-3 with Blackpool's Stan Mortensen scoring a hat-trick.
May 11th	A Category F5 tornado hits the town of Waco, Texas, causing mass destruction and leaving 115 people dead in its wake.
May 14th	US pilot Edwin "Buzz" Aldrin flying a North American F-86 Sabre, shoots down a MiG- 15 fighter during the Korean War. The pilot of the MiG ejects from the aircraft.
May 14th	The passenger liners SS Arcadia and SS Orsova are launched from Clydebank and Barrow-in-Furness respectively.
May 16th	American racing driver Chet Miller dies as a result of a crash in practice for the Indianapolis 500.
May 18th	In the skies above Rogers Dry Lake, California, pilot Jacqueline Cochlan, becomes the first woman to break the sound barrier in a North American F-86 Sabre.
May 25th	The first public television station in the USA officially begins broadcasting as KUHT from the campus of the University of Houston.
May 28th	In the Korean War the Battle of the Hook begins in Northern Korea. It is fought primarily between British and Chinese forces.
May 29th	Sir Edmund Hillary, from New Zealand and Sherpa Tenzing Norgay, from Nepal become the first men to reach the summit of Mount Everest.

Jun 2nd	People gather from around the World to attend the Coronation of Her Majesty Queen Elizabeth II. People also gather around their television sets as the Coronation is televised live at the insistence of the Queen.
Jun 9th	In the United States, CIA director secretly approves the use of the drug LSD in the interrogation of suspects.
Jun 10th	De facto Deputy British Prime Minister Anthony Eden undergoes a biliary tract operation, carried out at the New England Baptist Hospital in Boston, Massachusetts.
Jun 16th	Civil disorder breaks out in Communist East Germany. Strike action by construction workers begins in East Berlin, leading to a wider uprising against the government.
Jun 17th	The so-called "East German Uprising of 1953" is brutally suppressed by Soviet (Russian) forces.
Jun 18th	A United States Air Force Douglas C-124 Globemaster II crashes just after take-off from Tachikawa Airfield near Tokyo, Japan, killing all 129 people on board in the worst air crash in history to date and the first with a confirmed death toll exceeding 100.
Jun 19th	An African-American boycott of buses in Baton Rouge, Louisiana, begins. It heralds the beginning of the Civil Rights Movement in America.
Jun 22nd	The Government of Nepal hosts a reception for members of the Mount Everest Expedition, at which Tenzing Norgay is presented with a prize of ten thousand rupees, while Edmund Hillary and John Hunt are given jewelled Kukri (short swords). The Government of India announces the creation of a new Gold Medal for civilian gallantry, of which Hunt, Hillary and Tenzing are to be the first recipients.
Jun 30th	The first Colditz escapee and Nuremberg prosecutor Airey Neave is elected to parliament as MP for Abingdon.
Jun 30th	The first Chevrolet Corvette rolls off the production line in Flint, Michigan.

Jun 30th The first roll-on/roll off ferry leaves the Port of Dover headed for Boulogne, France.

Jul 3rd The first ascent of Nanga Parbat in the Pakistan Himalayas, the world's ninth highest mountain, is made by Austrian climber Hermann Buhl alone on an Austrian-German expedition.

Jul 4th The Wimbledon Tennis Championships end when Vic Seixas (USA) defeats Kurt Neilsen (Denmark) 9-7 6-3 6-4 in the men's singles final.

Jul 7th Harry Eyre, a novice speedway rider, dies of injuries sustained in a crash at West Ham Stadium during the 1953 Speedway National League season.

Jul 9th Arsonist Stanford Pattan starts the "Rattlesnake Fire" in the Mendocino National Forest in Northern California. One forest ranger and 14 volunteer firefighters are killed before the fire is brought under control.

Jul 16th Hilaire Belloc, the French-born English poet, novelist and historian dies aged 82.

Jul 26th The Short Creek Raid is carried out on a polygynous Mormon sect in Arizona, United States. It is thought to be the largest mass arrest of men and women in modern American history.

Jul 27th The Korean war ends with the Korean Armistice Agreement between the United Nations Command and the Communists represented by the People's Republic of China. It brings to an end more that three years of bloody fighting, which claimed the lives of between two and three million civilians and combatants. It is agreed that the North should remain communist and the South capitalist. No formal Peace Treaty is signed.

Aug 1st Indian Airlines, based in Delhi, begins operations, having been set up by a merger of regional airlines.

Aug 5th Operation "Big Switch" begins. In Korea The United Nations (UNC) repatriates 75,000 North Korean and Chinese prisoners of war, whilst the communists hand over almost 13,000 UNC POWs in return.

Aug 8th	37 people are injured when a northbound Royal Scot train is derailed near Abingdon in Scotland. The track had buckled as a result of unusually high temperatures.
Aug 10th	In an act of selfless heroism, mountaineer Pete Schoening saves the lives of five members of the American K2 expedition in the Himalayas.
Aug 12th	A magnitude 7.2 earthquake devastates most of the Ionian Sea islands in Greece's worst natural disaster in centuries.
Aug 15th	Ten people are killed in a train crash at Collyhurst near Manchester.
Aug 19th	The CIA and UK security services are involved in overthrowing the government of Mohammad Mosaddeg in Iran, so as to retain power for Shah Mohammad Reza Pahlavi.
Aug 20th	Seventeen U,S. Air Force F-84G Thunderjets make the longest ever non-stop flight by jet fighters. They travel from the United States to the United Kingdom by using aerial refueling.
Sep 5th	The Queen and the Duke of Edinburgh attend the Braemar Gathering, the most important of the Highland Games.
Sep 6th	Konrad Adenaeur's coalition retain power in West Germany's federal election. They now control two thirds of the Bundestag (lower house).
Sep 12th	U.S. Senator John Fitzgerald Kennedy marries Jacqueline Lee Bouvier in a ceremony at St. Mary's Church in Newport, Rhode Island
Sep 17th	After the death of the sitting MP Seymour Cocks, a by-election is held in the Nottinghamshire seat of Broxtowe. The less humorously named Will Warbey holds the seat for Labour.
Sep 21st	A North Korean pilot, No Kum-Sok, defects to South Korea. He receives a reward that had been offered by the U.S. Far East Command for the delivery of an intact MiG-15 fighter plane.
Sep 26th	Tea with two sugars is back on the menu as sugar rationing ends in the UK.

Sep 29th	The British Navy destroyer HMS Tyrian runs aground in the North Sea off Cromer, Norfolk. It is later refloated.
Oct 1st	The United States and South Korea sign a mutual defence treaty in Washington, D.C.
Oct 3rd	The Ryder Cup golf tournament, held at Wentworth Club in Virginia Water, Surrey ends in a sixth consecutive victory for the United States over Great Britain and Ireland.
Oct 6th	The United Nations Children's Fund (UNICEF), is made a permanent specialised agency of the United Nations.
Oct 9th	In a papal address Pope Pius XII delivers "The Technician", a document instructing scientists to restrict themselves to the study of physical matter and not to undermine the idea of a non-material soul or a Superior Being.
Oct 10th	British pilot Monty Burton wins the London to Christchurch air race (held to celebrate the centenary of Christchurch, New Zealand) in under 23 hours flying time.
Oct 18th	Peter Brook's live television production of *King Lear*, starring Orson Welles, is broadcast by CBS in America, It is part of a series called *Omnibus*, hosted by Alistair Cooke.
Oct 27th	The lifeboat Robert Lindsay, out of Arbroath, Scotland, capsizes after being hit by a freak wave and flung onto the rocks at Inchcape Park. Six crew members are killed.
Nov 11th	The current affairs series *Panorama* first airs on the BBC Television Service.
Nov 20th	The Douglas D-588-2 Skyrocket, piloted by Scott Crossfield, becomes the first manned aircraft to reach Mach 2 (twice the speed of sound).
Nov 20th	Boffins at London's Natural History Museum announce that the skull of Piltdown Man (allegedly an early human, "discovered" in 1912) is a hoax.
Nov 21st	The world's southernmost settlement, Puerto Williams (Chile), is founded.

Nov 26th The House of Lords backs Government plans for the introduction of commercial television in the UK.

Dec 2nd The BBC broadcasts its "Television Symbol" for the first time. It is the first animated television presentation symbol in the world. To many it looks like a set of bats' wings.

Dec 7th A visit to Iran by American Vice President Richard Nixon causes riots, as a reaction to the U.S. backing the overthrow of the government in August. Three students are shot dead by police in Tehran.

Dec 10th The Nobel Prizes are awarded in Stockholm, Sweden. Albert Schweitzer of France is awarded the Peace Prize and Winston Churchill is awarded the prize for Literature.

Dec 24th A railway bridge collapses at Tangiwai, New Zealand, sending a fully loaded passenger train into the Whangaehu River. 151 people are killed.

Dec 25th The Queen's Christmas message is broadcast to the nation. She recorded it during a tour of New Zealand. In it she states "Last Christmas I spoke to you from England; this year I am doing so from New Zealand. Auckland, which I reached only two days ago, is, I suppose, as far as any city in the world from London, and I have travelled some thousands of miles through many changing scenes and climates on my voyage here. Despite all that, however, I find myself today completely and most happily at home. Of course, we all want our children at Christmas time - for that is the season above all others when each family gathers at its own hearth. I hope that perhaps mine are listening to me now and I am sure that when the time comes they, too, will be great travellers." She continued…"Before we end this great journey we shall catch a glimpse of other places in Asia, Africa and in the Mediterranean. But what is really important to me is that I set out on this journey in order to see as much as possible of the people and countries of the Commonwealth and Empire, to learn at first hand something of their triumphs and difficulties and something of their hopes and fears. At the same time I want to show that the Crown is not merely an abstract symbol of our unity but a personal and living bond between you and me."

The Coronation of Queen Elizabeth II

An official portrait by Cecil Beaton

Proceeding past the Coronation Chair

Churchill with his son and grandson

Queen Elizabeth II was only 25 years old at the time of her Coronation, making her the youngest monarch to be crowned in British history. Her coronation took place on 2nd June 1953 at Westminster Abbey in London. The ceremony was attended by representatives from over 120 countries as well as thousands of guests from the United Kingdom and the Commonwealth making it the first major international event of the post-World War II era.

The event was broadcast on television and radio, making it the first coronation to be televised and allowing millions of people around the world to watch it live. In fact it led to a surge in sales of televisions. If people did not have a television they would go to a relative or neighbour who had one. The event marked a major shift in British broadcasting. More than 20 million people watched the service on television, outnumbering the radio audience for the first time. The BBC knew the event would be popular, based on the reaction to the limited broadcast of George VI's Coronation Procession, but did not foresee that it would mark the coming of age of television, as well as the modernisation of the monarchy.

The day began with the procession of the Queen and the royal family from Buckingham Palace to Westminster Abbey. The Queen was accompanied by her husband, Prince Philip, Duke of Edinburgh and her two children, Prince Charles and Princess Anne. They rode in the State Coach, a magnificent gold-plated carriage built for King George III in 1762. The procession was led by the King's Troop, Royal Horse Artillery and the Household Cavalry and included representatives from the armed forces and various charitable organisations for which she was patron. Upon arriving at Westminster Abbey, the Queen was greeted by the Dean of Westminster and the Archbishop of Canterbury, who led her to the Coronation Chair. The chair, which was made in 1300, is where the monarch sits during the coronation ceremony. The Queen then took her seat on the chair and the ceremony began with the singing of the National Anthem, “God Save The Queen”.

The coronation itself was a traditional Christian ceremony, filled with ancient rituals and symbolic gestures. The Queen was anointed with holy oil and the archbishop placed the crown on her head. She then took the oath, in which she pledged to govern the country according to its laws and customs. In all the ceremony took over three hours to complete.

After the ceremony, the Queen and the royal family returned to Buckingham Palace, where they appeared on the balcony to wave to the crowds gathered outside. The day ended with a reception at Buckingham Palace, where the Queen greeted guests from around the world. The coronation of Queen Elizabeth II was a grand and historic event that marked the beginning of her long and successful reign as the Queen of the United Kingdom and the Commonwealth.

It was also a significant moment in the history of television, as it was the first time that such a major event was broadcast live, allowing millions of people around the world to witness it. Elizabeth II brought stability to the monarchy and was a feature of all our lives until her death on September 8th 2022.

Interesting fact: Florist Constance Spry invented the now popular dish of Coronation Chicken as food for foreign guests, who were to be entertained after the coronation.

An Official Portrait by Cecil Beaton

The royal family gathered on the balcony at Buckingham Palace

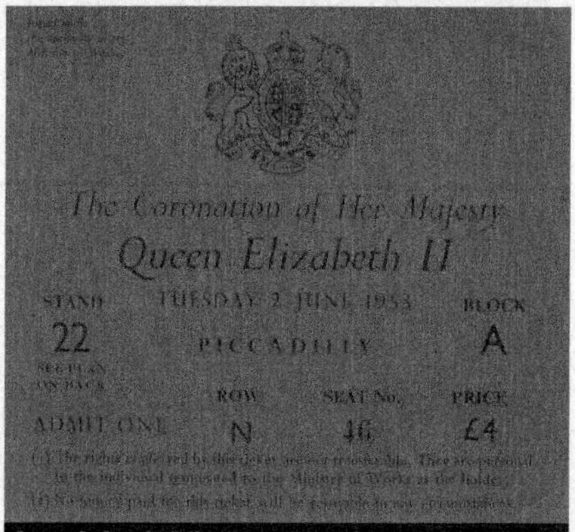

An original ticket to attend

Street parties took place throughout the UK

Waving from the balcony

The Crown Jewels

Sir Anthony Charles Lynton Blair KG

born on 6th May 1953 in Edinburgh, Scotland, UK

Tony Blair was Prime Minister of the United Kingdom from 1997 to 2007. He was the leader of the Labour Party and the youngest Prime Minister in the 20th century when he took office at the age of 43. His time in office was marked by many positive achievements, including the devolution of power to Scotland and Wales, the introduction of the minimum wage, and major investment in public services such as the National Health Service and education. He also played a key role in the international community, particularly in the fight against global terrorism. His most controversial move was the decision to join the US-led invasion of Iraq in 2003. Despite the fact that there were no weapons of mass destruction found there, Blair insisted that the invasion was necessary to remove Saddam Hussein and to spread democracy in the region. This decision remains highly contentious and was a major factor in his declining popularity. Because of this controversy, Blair's legacy as Prime Minister is mixed. On the one hand, he is credited with modernising the Labour Party and making it a credible and electable force. On the other, many feel that his support for the Iraq war and his close relationship with US President George W. Bush damaged the UK's reputation and undermined its position in the world.

While at Oxford University Blair was the lead singer of a band called Ugly Rumours.

Pierce Brendan Brosnan OBE

born on 16th May 1953 in Drogheda, County Louth, Ireland

Brosnan is an actor, film producer and environmentalist best known for his role as James Bond in four films from 1995 to 2002. He was raised in London after his father abandoned the family when he was an infant. He started his acting career in the 1970s and became a popular television star in the 80s with his role as *Remington Steele*. In 1995, He was selected to replace Timothy Dalton as James Bond, starring in four films: *GoldenEye*, *Tomorrow Never Dies*, *The World is Not Enough* and *Die Another Day*. He received widespread critical acclaim for his performances as the suave and sophisticated British spy. He has been referred to as one of the best James Bond actors of all time. Aside from James Bond, he has appeared in numerous other films including *The Thomas Crown Affair*, *Mamma Mia!* and *Love is All You Need*. He has also lent his voice to animated films such as *The SpongeBob SquarePants Movie* and *Thomas & Friends*. Brosnan is also known for his humanitarian work, being a Goodwill Ambassador for UNICEF and a strong advocate for environmental issues. He is a supporter of various charities and is a member of the board of directors for the World Wildlife Fund. In addition to his acting career, Brosnan is also a talented painter and has published a book of his works.

Brosnan's first film role was a nameless part in 1980's *The Long Good Friday*. Simply credited as 1st Irishman, he is seen at the end of the movie holding Harold Shand (Bob Hoskins) at gunpoint in the back of a car.

Victoria Wood CBE

born on 19th May 1953 in Prestwich, Lancashire, UK

Wood was a British comedian, actor, singer and songwriter known for her observational comedy and satire. She began her career as a stand-up comedian in the 1970s, later moving to television and film. Wood was particularly known for her ability to poke fun at everyday life and societal norms in a relatable and clever way. She often wrote and starred in her own material, including the popular TV series *Victoria Wood: As Seen on TV* and *Dinnerladies*. In addition to her comedic work, Wood was also a talented singer and songwriter. She released several albums throughout her career, including *Victoria Wood* and *Coast to Coast* and wrote songs for several of her TV shows and films. Wood received numerous awards throughout her career, including five BAFTA's, two British Comedy Awards and a Special Prize at the Montreux Comedy Festival. In addition to her on-stage and screen performances, Wood was also known for her charitable work. She was a patron of the Teenage Cancer Trust and a supporter of various other charities, and would often perform at fundraising events. Victoria Wood passed away in 2016, but her comedy and music continue to be loved by audiences of all ages. Her wit, observational humour and clever songwriting have cemented her place as a comedic legend in the UK. She was also the most generous of writers, often giving her fellow actors the best lines.

"In my day we didn't have sex education, we just picked up what we could off the television... and as far as I was concerned, if Pinky and Perky didn't do it, I didn't want to know about it."

Michael Denzil Xavier Portillo MBE

born on 26th May 1953 in Bushey, Hertfordshire, UK

Michael Portillo is a British politician, journalist and broadcaster. He served as a Member of Parliament for the Conservative Party from 1984 to 1997 and again from 1999 to 2005 and held various positions in the government of Prime Minister John Major, including Minister of State for Transport and Chief Secretary to the Treasury. In 2001, Portillo stood for the leadership of the Conservative Party following the resignation of William Hague, but lost to Iain Duncan Smith. He later returned to the Conservative front bench as Shadow Chancellor of the Exchequer, but resigned from Parliament in 2005 and pursued a career in journalism and broadcasting. Portillo has presented a number of documentaries on historical and political subjects, including the popular series *Great British Railway Journeys* and Portillo's *Hidden History of Britain*. He is also a regular contributor to various newspapers and magazines, including The Times and The Spectator. He is a Fellow of the Royal Society of Arts and a Fellow of the Royal Geographical Society. He has served as a Trustee of the Imperial War Museum and the National Portrait Gallery. In 2018 he accepted the role as President of the Friends of the Settle-Carlisle Railway. He has been recognised for his ability to be self-deprecating and candid, even when discussing his own political failures.

Portillo, a conservative, grew up in a left-wing family. His father was active in the Spanish Civil War and fled Spain in 1939 when the fascist regime of General Franco seized control.

Kathleen Kennedy

born on 5th June 1953 in Berkeley, California, USA

Kathleen Kennedy is an American film producer who has been active in the entertainment industry for over four decades. She is best known for her work with director Steven Spielberg and as a co-founder of Amblin Entertainment and The Kennedy/Marshall Company. Kennedy has produced some of the most iconic films of our time, including the *Indiana Jones* franchise, *Jurassic Park*, *E.T. the Extra-Terrestrial* and the *Back to the Future* trilogy. Born in Berkeley, California, Kennedy attended San Diego State University, where she studied communication and film. After graduation, she began working in television and went on to work on numerous productions, including *The Money Pit* and *Poltergeist*. In 1982, she co-founded Amblin Entertainment with Spielberg and Frank Marshall. The company went on to produce some of the most successful films in Hollywood. She has received numerous awards, including the Irving G. Thalberg Memorial Award from the Academy of Motion Picture Arts and Sciences, the Producers' Guild of America's David O. Selznick Achievement Award and the Women in Film Crystal Award. In 2012, Kennedy became the President of Lucasfilm and was responsible for the revival of the Star Wars franchise with the release of the critically acclaimed film *Star Wars: The Force Awakens*. Under her leadership, the company has continued to produce new films in the *Star Wars* universe, including *Rogue One: A Star Wars Story*.

Kennedy has one uncredited role in front of the cameras when she played a missionary in *Indiana Jones and the Temple of Doom* (1984).

Benazir Bhutto

born on 21st June 1953 in Karachi, Pakistan

Bhutto followed her father into politics and both of them died because of it. He was executed in 1979. Her two brothers also suffered violent deaths. Like the Nehru-Gandhi family in India, the Bhuttos of Pakistan are one of the world's most famous political dynasties. She was educated at Harvard and Oxford and gained credibility from her father's high profile, even though she was a reluctant entrant into politics. She was twice prime minister of Pakistan, from 1988 to 1990 and from 1993 to 1996. At the height of her popularity, shortly after her first election win, she was one of the most high-profile women leaders in the world. Young and glamorous, she successfully portrayed herself as a refreshing contrast to the overwhelmingly male-dominated political establishment. Ms. Bhutto was imprisoned just before her father's death and spent most of her five-year jail term in solitary confinement. She described the conditions as extremely harsh. During stints out of prison for medical treatment, Ms Bhutto set up a Pakistan People's Party office in London and began a campaign against the incumbent General Zia. She returned to Pakistan in 1986, attracting huge crowds to political rallies. After Zia died in an explosion on board his aircraft in 1988, she became the first democratically elected female prime ministers in an Islamic country. She was murdered by the Pakistani Taliban on 27th December 2007 after which her country was once more plunged into chaos.

Bhutto was the first elected female leader to give birth while in office. The second was Jacinda Adern of New Zealand.

Cynthia Ann Stephanie Lauper Thornton

born on 22nd June 1953 in New York City, USA

Cindy Lauper is an American singer, songwriter, and actress. She first rose to fame in the 1980s with her debut album *She's So Unusual*, which produced the hit singles *Girls Just Want to Have Fun* and *Time After Time*. The album was a commercial success, selling over six million copies in the United States and earning Lauper a Grammy Award for Best New Artist. Throughout her career, she has released several more albums and had several hit singles, including *True Colors*, and *I Drove All Night*. In addition to her music career, she has also acted in films and television shows, including *Vibes*, *Life with Mikey* and *Mad About You*. She is known for her distinctive style and unique voice, and has been cited as an influence by many other musicians. She has also been involved in various philanthropic causes, including LGBTQ rights and animal rights. In 2013, She received the Stephen F. Kolzak Award from the Gay and Lesbian Alliance Against Discrimination. In addition, Lauper has written a musical, *Kinky Boots*, which was based on the 2005 British film of the same name. The musical premiered on Broadway in 2013 and won six Tony Awards, including Best Musical.

This quote from her best sums up her outlook on life. "You always have to remember, no matter what you're told, that God loves all the flowers. Even the wild ones that grow on the side of the highway"

Graham Alan Gooch OBE, DL

born on 23rd July 1953 in Whipps Cross, Essex, UK

Gooch is a former English cricketer who is widely considered to be one of the greatest opening batsmen of all time. He played for Essex and England, and captained both teams. He made his debut for Essex in 1973 and for England in 1975. He played for England until 1995 and at the time of his retirement was the leading run-scorer in Test match cricket for England. He was known for his technical proficiency and his ability to score runs in all conditions. He scored over 100 first-class centuries in his career and is the only player to score a century in both innings of a Test match three times. He also captained England in 34 Test matches, leading the team to victory in 15 of them. In addition to his success on the field, he is also known for his work as a coach. He has coached Essex, England and many other teams, and has helped to develop many young players. Gooch has also been involved in the media as a commentator and analyst and has written several books about cricket. Despite his success, Gooch had to deal with several controversies during his career. He was involved in a match-fixing scandal in the late 1990s, but was cleared of any wrongdoing. He was also criticised for his captaincy style and for his role in the "Rebel Tours" to South Africa during the Apartheid era.

Gooch holds the record for most runs scored in a single test match. Against India at Lords in 1990, he scored 333 in the first innings and 123 in the second.

Nigel Ernest James Mansell OBE

born on 8th August 1953 in Upton-upon-Severn, Worcs, UK

Nigel Mansell was a former Formula One racing driver. He began his F1 career in 1980 with the Lotus team and quickly established himself as a competitive driver, winning his first Grand Prix in 1985. In 1986, he joined the Williams team and won the World Championship the following year with a then record number of wins in a single season. He also won the Championship in 1992. During his F1 career, he achieved 31 Grand Prix wins and 32 pole positions. He is considered one of the greatest drivers in the history of Formula One. Mansell was known for his aggressive driving style and his fierce competitiveness on the track. He was often involved in on-track battles with other drivers, particularly Ayrton Senna and Alain Prost. Off the track, he was also known for his charismatic personality and his passionate fan base. After retiring from Formula One in 1995, he competed in various other motorsports, including IndyCar and the Le Mans 24 Hour race. He also made several one-off appearances in F1, including taking part in the 1999 British Grand Prix at the age of 48. Throughout his career, he received several awards and honours, including the BBC Sports Personality of the Year in 1992. He was inducted into the International Motorsports Hall of Fame in 2005 and was appointed a Member of the Order of the British Empire in 1986.

During his racing career Mansell lived on the Isle of Man, where he served as a special constable.

James "Midge" Ure OBE

born on 10th October 1953 in Cambuslang, Scotland, UK

Ure is a Scottish singer, songwriter and musician who rose to fame as the lead vocalist of the new wave band Ultravox. He started his musical career in the 1970s as a member of several rock bands, including Slik and Visage, before joining Ultravox in 1979. With the band, he achieved international success and recognition for their innovative blend of electronic music and rock. His work with Ultravox is regarded as some of the most influential music of the 1980s. Their fourth studio album, *Vienna* (1980), which was co-written and co-produced by Ure, reached the number two spot in the UK charts and spawned the hit single *Vienna*, which topped the charts in several countries. He also wrote and produced several other hit singles with Ultravox, including *Dancing with Tears in My Eyes* and *Reap the Wild Wind*. After leaving Ultravox in 1986, he went on to pursue a solo career, releasing several critically acclaimed albums and hit singles, including *If I Was* and *Breathe*. He also became involved in charity work, co-organising the groundbreaking charity event Live Aid in 1985, which raised millions of pounds for famine relief in Africa. He has continued to tour and record music throughout his career, and has collaborated with many other musicians and artists. He has been recognised for his contributions to music and charity, receiving several awards and accolades, including an Ivor Novello Award and an OBE.

Ure's signature song, Vienna, peaked at number 2 in the UK charts. It was held off the number one slot by Joe Dolce's novelty record *Shaddup You Face*.

Griffith "Griff" Rhys Jones OBE

born on 16th November 1953 in Cardiff, Wales, UK

Griff Rhys Jones is a Welsh comedian, writer and actor. He is best known for his work as a performer on the BBC sketch comedy series *Not the Nine O'Clock News* and *Alas Smith and Jones*. (the show's title being a pun on the American television series *Alias Smith and Jones*). Rhys Jones has also appeared in numerous British television shows and films, including *The Young Ones*, *A Bit of Fry & Laurie*, *Three Men in a Boat*, and *Mount Pleasant*. In 1981, Rhys Jones along with Mel Smith founded Talkback, a production company which produced many British comedy series, including, *Smack the Pony*, *Da Ali G Show*, *I'm Alan Partridge*, *They Think Its All Over*, *QI* and *Big Train*. Outside of his acting career, he is also a passionate travel writer and presenter. He has presented a number of travel documentaries for the BBC, including *Griff Rhys Jones: Rivers* and *Griff Rhys Jones: Lost Kingdoms of Africa*. In these programmes, he explores the history and culture of different regions, often with a focus on the natural environment. He is also an active campaigner for environmental and conservation issues. He is a patron of the Woodland Trust and has spoken out against the impact of development on Britain's green spaces. In addition, he has been involved in campaigns to protect the Welsh language and to preserve the traditional architecture of the Wales.

"We need a corrective on who is a genuine artist. I'm an opportunist. I have no talent. That's true of 99 per cent of people in the British media. Graham and Arthur who wrote *Father Ted* or Armando Iannucci are God-like as they have talent. Everyone else is a drone."

Christina Hambley Brown, Lady Evans CBE

born on 21st November 1953 in Maidenhead, Berkshire, UK

Tina Brown is a British journalist, editor and media executive. She is best known for her work as the editor-in-chief of *Tatler*, *Vanity Fair* and *The New Yorker*. Brown began her career in journalism as a reporter for *The Sunday Times*, where she quickly rose through the ranks to become the paper's youngest ever editor at the age of 25. In 1983, she was appointed the editor-in-chief of *Tatler*, a British society magazine and turned it into a widely-read and influential publication. In 1984, Brown moved to New York to take over as editor-in-chief of *Vanity Fair*. During her tenure at the magazine, she made it a must-read for the cultural elite with her mix of high-profile interviews, investigative journalism and celebrity profiles. In 1992, she left *Vanity Fair* to become the editor-in-chief of *The New Yorker*, where she served until 1998. Under her leadership, the magazine's circulation and advertising revenues increased and it won numerous awards for journalistic excellence. Brown has also been involved in several other media ventures, including founding Talk, a magazine and media company and serving as the CEO of *The Daily Beast*, a news website. She is a frequent commentator on media and cultural issues, and has written several books, including *The Diana Chronicles* and *Tina Brown Live Media*.

Brown was expelled from three boarding schools, the third time for writing an essay in which the school was blown up and replaced by a public lavatory.

Franz Klammer

born on 3rd December 1953 in Mooswald, Carinthia, Austria

Klammer is a retired Alpine skier who specialised in the downhill event, winning 25 World Cup downhill races in his career. His golden years were 1975 and 1976. In 1975 he won an astonishing eight of the nine downhill World Cup races, which made him favourite for the event at the 1976 Winter Olympics held at Innsbruck in his native Austria. This added to the pressure on him and he also faced defending Olympic champion, Bernhard Russi of Switzerland. Skiing close to last, Klammer gave one of the most thrilling performances in the history of the Winter Games. Partway down the run he trailed Russi by a fraction of a second, but he skied with such wild abandon over the final 1,000m that he seemed almost on the verge of a dangerous fall. When he crossed the finish line he had won the gold by only one-third of a second. Holder of the World Cup downhill title from 1975 to 1978 and again in 1983, Klammer also won a gold medal in the Alpine combination and a silver medal in the downhill at the 1974 World Championships. He was named Austrian Sportsman of the Year three times in 1975, 1976 and 1983.

Immediately after his retirement from alpine competition, he took up motor racing, and was soon involved in touring car racing, driving Mercedes-Benz saloons all over Europe and racing professionally as far away as Australia. In 1990, he won a round of the prestigious European Touring Car Championship.

John Malkovich

born on 9th December 1953 in Christopher, Illinois, USA

John Malkovich is an American actor, director, and fashion designer who is widely regarded as one of the greatest and most versatile actors of his generation. Malkovich began acting in local theatre productions before moving to New York City in 1976 to further his career in acting. Over the course of his career, he has appeared in numerous films, television shows and stage productions, earning critical acclaim and accolades for his performances. His breakthrough role came in the 1987 film *Places in the Heart*, for which he earned an Academy Award nomination for Best Supporting Actor. He went on to appear in numerous other successful films, including *Dangerous Liaisons*, *Being John Malkovich*, *Burn After Reading* and *Red*. He is also known for his work on stage, having performed in a number of productions both on-and off-Broadway, and for his directorial efforts, including the films *The Dancer Upstairs* and *Hidden Sun*. In addition to his acting career, Malkovich is also known for his involvement in the fashion industry. He has collaborated with several fashion designers and brands, and in 2010, launched his own fashion line, Technobohemian. Malkovich's unique style and versatility as an actor have made him one of the most respected and sought-after performers in the entertainment industry.

"I still don't know if I made the right decision when I went into acting. I have driven school buses, sold egg rolls and painted houses, and I have often wondered what my life would have been like if I hadn't gone into acting. Mind you, it's a great life, going around pretending you're other people and getting paid ridiculous sums of money for it."

Sir Mark Trevor Phillips OBE ARCS FIC

born on 31st December 1953 in Islington, London, UK

Trevor Phillips is a British journalist, writer and television presenter. He is best known for his work as a presenter and commentator on British television, where he has covered a wide range of social and political issues. He has presented programmes such as *The London Programme*, *Panorama* and *Dispatches*. Much of his work places a particular emphasis on race and diversity in British society. He has written extensively on these topics and has been a vocal advocate for greater equality and inclusion. He served as the Chair of the Equality and Human Rights Commission from 2003 to 2012, where he worked to promote and protect the rights of minority groups in the UK. In addition to his journalism and activism, Phillips is also a prolific writer. He has written several books on race, diversity and social justice, including *Windrush: The Irresistible Rise of Multi-Racial Britain* and *The Tri-racial Isolates of Britain: An Interim Report*. He has also written columns and opinion pieces for various newspapers and magazines. Throughout his career, Phillips has been recognised for his contributions to British society and culture. He has received numerous awards and honours, including the OBE for services to race equality in 2000, and the Lifetime Achievement Award from the Institute of Race Relations in 2011. He was Knighted in 2022 for his services to equality and human rights.

Phillips and ex-London Mayor Ken Livingstone have had a long-running feud. Phillips is reported to have said "I ask questions, and a large part of my life has been spent asking questions of Ken Livingstone."

Other Notable Births

Nigel Planer
22nd February 1953
Actor | Writer

Michael Bolton
26th February 1953
Singer | Songwriter

Isabelle Huppert
16th March 1953
Actress

Chaka Khan
23rd March 1953
Singer

Rick Moranis
18th April 1953
Actor | Comedian

Ruby Wax
19th April 1953
Actress | Comedian

Sebastian Faulks
20th April 1953
Novelist | Journalist

Mike Oldfield
15th May 1953
Musician | Songwriter

Alfred Molina
24th May 1953
Actor

Tim Allen
13th June 1953
Actor | Comedian

Hulk Hogan
11th August 1953
Wrestler

Roger Allam
26th October 1953
Actor

Kim Basinger
8th December 1953
Actress | Model

Bill Pullman
17th December 1953
Actor

Richard Clayderman
28th December 1953
Pianist

Joseph Vissarionovich Stalin

died aged 74 on 5th March 1953 in Moscow, Soviet Union

Josef Stalin was a monstrous tyrant who seized complete control of the Soviet Union shortly after the death of Lenin. He was loathed and worshipped by the Russian population in equal measure, but such was the fist of iron that he ruled with, those who hated him had to pretend to worship him. Throughout his career, he sought to stifle debate and opposition, largely through murder. Many in Russia saw him as a great saviour, rescuing his country from conquest by Nazi Germany. The truth however was different. His purges of the communist party and military between 1935-8 left Russia bereft of military leadership. It was only by chance that his greatest General, Zhukov, survived. The most telling story about Stalin occurred during the 1945 victory parade. Stalin was due to ride a white stallion, but was thrown off it in rehearsal. He instructed Zhukov to ride the tempestuous horse instead. He did this with aplomb, saluting Stalin in the process.

Arthur "Dooley" Wilson

died aged 67 on 30th May 1953 in Los Angeles, California, USA

Dooley was born Arthur Wilson in Tyler, Texas. His exact year of birth was debated for years, listed in reference books as either 1886 or 1894. His grave marker, however, at Angelus Rosedale Cemetery in Los Angeles gives the year 1886. At age 12, he performed in minstrel shows and later became a fixture in black theatre in both Chicago and New York (circa 1908). He received the nickname "Dooley" while working in the Pekin Theatre in Chicago, because of his then-signature Irish song *Mr. Dooley*, which he usually performed in whiteface as an Irishman. In subsequent years Dooley displayed his musical skills in various forms. As a vaudevillian, drummer and jazz band leader, he entertained both in the US and in 1920s Europe, playing in London and Paris. From the 1930s to the 1950s he focused on theatrical musicals and occasional films. He is however remembered above all for one song – his rendition of *As Time Goes By*, as the character Sam, in the 1942 film *Casablanca*.

Edwin Hubble

died aged 63 on 28th September 1953 in San Marino, California,USA

Born on 20th November 1889 in Marshfield, Missouri, Hubble spent his youth honing athletic skills while mentally feeding his curiosity through science fiction novels. Hubble's innate fascination with the world foretold a lifetime of exploration. He earned a bachelor's degree in mathematics and astronomy from University of Chicago. He briefly deviated from his path of exploration, largely fuelled by his father's expectations, to study law at Oxford University as a Rhodes Scholar. But his deep longing to pursue a career in the sciences outweighed his father's hopes, and Hubble switched gears and obtained a PhD. in astronomy from the University of Chicago in 1914, setting his focus on the heavens. By 1929, Hubble had completely reimagined our place in the universe; not only was it home to millions of other galaxies, but the universe itself was expanding. Contrary to the previously held view of a static universe, Hubble ultimately proved that galaxies are, in fact, moving away from us. This was his greatest legacy.

Nigel Bruce

died aged 58 on 8th October 1953 in Santa Monica, California, USA

Nigel Bruce was a British actor known for his role as Dr. John Watson in the *Sherlock Holmes* film series of the 1940s. He was born on 14th December 1895, in Ensenada, Baja California, Mexico. He started his career on stage and made his first film appearance in 1917. He appeared in over 80 films in a career that spanned three decades. In addition to his role as Dr. Watson, Bruce also appeared in several other films, including *For Whom the Bell Tolls* (1943) and *Abbott and Costello Meet the Killer, Boris Karloff* (1949). His legacy as Dr. Watson in the Sherlock Holmes films continues to be celebrated to this day, and he is remembered as one of the great character actors of his time. He was known for his comedic timing and his ability to bring dry humour to his roles. He was also a talented musician and enjoyed playing the piano in his spare time.

Dylan Thomas

died aged 39 on 9th November 1953 in New York City, USA

Dylan Thomas is widely regarded as one of the 20th century's most influential poets. His work is known for its imaginative use of language and rich imagery. He wrote several collections, including *18 Poems* (1934) and *The Map of Love* (1939). He also wrote several plays for radio and stage including *Under Milk Wood* (1954), which is a fictionalised portrayal of a Welsh seaside village. He was known for his boisterous personality and love of drink, but his life was often marked by personal and financial struggles. He died aged just 39 after a drinking binge in New York City. His poems were often deeply personal exploring themes of love, death, and the meaning of life. He is particularly celebrated for his lyrical style and use of language, which is often characterised by musicality and sensory imagery. He was heavily influenced by the Romantic poets, as well as Welsh folklore and his own experiences growing up in Wales. Some of his most famous poems include *Do Not Go Gentle Into That Good Night* and *And Death Shall Have No Dominion*.

Eugene O'Neill

died aged 65 on 27th November 1953 in Boston, USA

O'Neill was an American playwright, considered one of the greatest of the 20th century. Born in New York City, he lived a life marked by personal turmoil and illness. He wrote 44 plays, including *Long Day's Journey Into Night*, *The Iceman Cometh* and *Mourning Becomes Electra*. His works often dealt with themes of family, addiction and disillusionment, and are known for their powerful and realistic dialogue. He was awarded the Nobel Prize in Literature in 1936 and four of his plays won the Pulitzer Prize. His life and work were also shaped by his own experiences, including a tumultuous childhood, his time as a sailor and his struggles with addiction. He drew upon these experiences to create deeply introspective characters who are searching for meaning and purpose. O'Neill's ability to probe the human condition and his innovative use of dramatic techniques helped to revolutionise American theatre, making him a central figure in the development of modern American drama.

The Coins We Used

18 years before decimalisation, we used the system of **pounds**, **shillings** and **pence** commonly represented using the symbols **£sd**. The **£** symbol evolved over many years from the letter **L** which derives from the Latin word *libra*, meaning a pound of money. Although **s** is the first letter of the word shilling, the use of the letter derives from the Latin word *solidus* which means coin. The curious use of the letter **d** for pennies also has a Latin origin from the word *denarius* meaning containing ten. Unlike the decimal system based on multiples of 10, the pre-decimal system was based on multiples of 12. There were 12 pennies to a shilling and 240 pennies to a pound. This meant there were 20 shillings to the pound. In 1953 there were 9 coins in circulation with evocative names that still permeate our language today.

Farthing ¼ d
In use to 1961

With 4 farthings to a penny, these smallest of coins featured a smooth edge and a wren on the reverse. *He hasn't got two farthings to rub together* was a popular expression to describe someone poor.

Halfpenny ½ d
In use to 1969

Commonly known as the *ha'penny* it is was the only word in the English language with a silent 'f'. Since 1937 the coin featured Sir Francis Drake's ship The Golden Hind. The popular pub game *Shove Ha'penny* features 5 halfpennies.

Penny 1d
In use to 1971

Before 1860 the penny was a large copper coin. This is why bicycles with a large front wheel were nicknamed Penny Farthings. Popular expressions using the penny include *ten a penny* and *a penny for your thoughts*.

Threepence 3d
In use to 1971

These 12-sided coins were commonly known as *thruppence* or *thrupenny bits*. The silver versions known as *joeys* were often hidden in Christmas puddings making an exciting find for the lucky children who discovered them.

Sixpence 6d
In use to 1980

These silver coins reputedly brought good luck. Sixpences were placed in bride's shoes as a wedding gesture. Known as benders, they could easily be bent. *Going on a bender* derived from drinking all day in pubs with sixpence.

Shilling 1/-
In use to 1990

First minted in the reign of Henry VII as a testoon, the shilling was latterly commonly known as a bob. *Taking the king's shilling* meant enrolling in the army whilst *a few bob short of a pound* describes someone a bit dim.

Florin 2/-
In use to 1992

The florin was Britain's first decimal coin in response to calls in the mid 19th Century for decimal coinage to be introduced. As 2 bob, the florin was worth 1/10th of a pound. After decimalisation in 1971, florins became worth 10 pence.

Half Crown 2/6
In use to 1969

Half crowns were originally struck in gold in the reign of Henry VIII. The first silver half crowns were issued under Edward VI in 1549. Surviving for over 450 years, the half crown was one of the most successful coins of all time.

Crown 5/-
In use to present day

The British crown is a heavy silver coin. Rarely spent, crowns are often minted for commemorative purposes. After decimalisation a crown was worth 25p until 1990 when their face value was changed to £5.

The average annual wage in the UK in 1953 was approximately:

£375-£450

The Morris Minor was introduced in the UK in 1948. Designed by Alec Issigonis who would later go on to design the Mini, this series II Morris Minor launched in 1952 would cost approximately:

£600 - £650

The price of the average house would be approximately 5-6x the average annual wage. Depending on where you were in the country this meant the price of a typical 1930's 3-bedroom semi-detached house would be in the region of:

£1,750 - £2,250

The Bush TV22 television set had an iconic Bakelite design holding a 9" screen receiving only one channel. Very expensive for the average family, they cost:

£38 12s

In 1953 the average price of a large loaf of wholemeal bread was:

7½d

A gallon of petrol (which is equivalent to 4.5 litres) cost:

4s 6½d

National Service

National service recruits enjoying a cup of tea whilst off duty in a NAAFI

Indian and British soldiers in Korea

National Service was introduced in 1947 to overcome challenges and resolve military manpower shortages in the wake of World War II. Wartime conscription was extended into an obligatory period of National Service for men of military age. Over 2 million were called up to the armed forces, often serving in one of Britain's many colonial outposts around the world.

After passing a medical and joining up, all conscripts had six weeks of basic training during which they got used to military life. Once enlisted and inside camp National Servicemen were issued with their equipment, which often consisted of ill-fitting uniforms and boots. Conscripts were knocked into shape by sergeants under pressure to train them in as short a time as possible. Most conscripts lived in cold barracks with primitive toilets and washing facilities. The lucky few had newly built, brick barracks with central heating. Some were housed in a 'Barrack Spider' - a wooden hut with eight rooms and a central washing area. Up to twenty men were housed in each room. Each man had a steel wardrobe, an iron bed and a one-foot locker for small items of kit. Overseas accommodation varied a lot. Servicemen could find themselves sharing a tent with three other men, such as in camps in Cyprus, or even as many as 15, as in war-torn Korea.

The camps and accommodation for servicemen in the Suez Canal Zone were amongst the worst, but those in Germany were generally of a high standard. Recruits soon began the seemingly endless task of polishing kit and equipment. Many regarded this as mindless drill aimed at destroying individuality. However, this strict regime helped foster a group identity and brought recruits closer together with many lifelong friendships being formed. Officers who did four years or more on a Short Service Commission were allowed to train in a speciality. Many other ranks were trained in general clerical duties, such as typing. Some received more specific training in technical subjects, such as communications and engineering. Languages were also taught at the Joint Service School of Languages at Bodmin. Russian was especially useful in this Cold War era. For those stationed in war zones, the possibility of death was suddenly part of daily life. The experience many men had of being thrown into combat situations, such as in Korea, Malaysia and Egypt, would never be forgotten. Men with minimal training were expected to fight hardened guerrilla fighters or cope with riots or civil unrest. Between 1947 and 1963, a total of 395 National Servicemen were killed on active duty.

Office Life

The first thing that would strike you if you were transported back to a British office in 1953, is that there was very little plugged in to the wall. Virtually everything from typewriters to adding machines were manual. In large offices, the typing pool, which was almost universally staffed by women, was a noisy place. Correcting mistakes was done either by correction fluid or a ribbon, which necessitated the typist using a backspace key and retyping the offending letter or word thereby masking it. Often, letters would look a bit of a mess so accuracy was highly prized. Secretarial training was considered a good move for young women and gave them an income and financial freedom.

A state of the art office environment in 1953

An employee creating punch cards

For many it was a job to do before marriage and domestic life, and it was always a good skill to have as it gave them "something to fall back on". After marriage, work as a school secretary was sought after as it allowed married woman to continue working in the knowledge that their hours and holidays coincided with their children's. There were virtually no computers, in fact the term was more likely to describe a person than it was a machine. The photocopier, invented in the US, was still in development and was virtually no use at all. One copy would take up to fifteen minutes to produce, meaning that it was often quicker to have a secretary type the letter again. Larger offices were very regimented places. The managers, nearly all men, would have separate toilet facilities, dining rooms and in some places even lifts. The general staff, consisting of mainly female secretaries, maintenance men and messenger boys shared the general staff canteen, which was often a more fun place to be.

The glass ceiling for women, except in very rare cases, was reached when usually a more mature woman became a personal secretary to a manager. Along with all general clerical duties, she was charged with running the manager's schedule, organising and laying out meetings, attending to the diary, answering phone calls and especially on a Friday after many a manager had a liquid lunch, telling people that her boss was "currently indisposed." It would take decades for the British office to become more egalitarian places where staff were not employed on the basis of gender or the colours of an old school tie.

Secretaries hard at work in the typing pool

Life on the Farm

Farm machinery replaced work originally done by labourers

A family on their summer break helping with the harvest

Farming in Britain was in a state of great flux in 1953. A new age of mechanisation was dawning as the country emerged from the war years. Back then the call to "Dig for Victory" encouraged food production on every spare acre of land. Even in 1953, eight years after the end of the war, food shortages still prevailed with farming strictly controlled by the Government. The Journal of the Ministry of Agriculture announced that "The world food outlook is very grave indeed....a united effort on the part of scientists and farmers will be needed if the situation is to be saved". Farmers quickly noted that the ministry mentioned scientists first with this causing tension between those who worked the land and those who told them how to do it. Through subsidy and control the government encouraged the production of arable crops, milk, pork and eggs. This led to a marked increase in the price of other produce with food shortages still prevalent. Although mechanisation helped with the workload, most work was done by hand.

The life of a farm labourer was tough. Ploughing and harvesting were increasingly done by machine but such tasks as milking cows, digging drainage channels and bailing hay were done by hand. Farmers, as they do today, largely lived by the hours of daylight; harvest time in the Autumn was particularly arduous. In the summertime when fruit was at its most bountiful, families and teenage children travelled from the towns and cities to help with the harvest. A hangover from this persists to this day; it is the reason children are given six weeks' summer holiday. However, British kids should have been thankful that they did not grow up in Ireland where they had three months "holiday".

Famously, London schoolchildren were sent by coach to Kent to help with hop picking for the brewing industry. Many had fond memories of the experience, but most often living conditions were poor, pay was minimal and some yearned for the relative tranquillity of home and even school! For farmers, the highlight of the year, as it is today, was the country show. This was and is an age old celebration of all things rural. There were dances, food aplenty, tug of war contests between the rufty-tufty farmhands and the quaffing of large amounts of the local brew. These were also places where business was done and contests for the best livestock often resulted in the winner changing hands for a princely sum.

The Primary School

A game of marbles in the playground

In 1953 there were no state funded nurseries. For most children their early life centred around the home, cared for by a stay-at-home mother or other members of their extended family. Children entered school at the age of five and for many it was a big shock. Many tears were shed at the school gates as mothers loosened their grip both literally and metaphorically. The day would start with assembly and a roll-call, the register. Children would sit cross-legged on the floor and listen to an address from the headteacher which was followed by the singing of a hymn. It was then on to the classroom.

A lesson in how to hold the bat

Each pupil was assigned their own desk, this normally faced the front of the classroom. The desk had a flap with storage space underneath and an inkwell at its upper edge. Children were eased gently into school life and little was done on the first day. Upon returning home many were surprised to find out that they had to do it again the next day. When lessons became serious there was much emphasis on the "three Rs": reading, writing and arithmetic. This immediately confused many as only one of the subjects actually began with R. Reading often involved reciting poetry or prose from memory or reading passages of a book aloud. Writing was not only a test of spelling and grammar, but also of handwriting skills. Pupils normally wrote in pencil except when they were taught rudimentary calligraphy. Some fared better than others and the skills learned stayed with them through to adulthood.

For others it was torture as each pupil was at the mercy of the children who had used the nib pen before them. Each pen was worn down in different ways and this bias was particularly difficult for left-handers. Arithmetic (maths) involved learning the times table, usually up to the number 12. The Britain of the day was pre-decimal and had 12 pennies to a shilling so knowing how to count in twelves was useful. There were few gizmos, the teacher stood at the front of the class and wrote on a blackboard. The pupils would have little more than a geometry set consisting of a set square, a protractor, a metal compass, a pencil and sharpener and a stencil. Other than the pencil most items were rarely used.

Children at a primary school in Wales

There was also music and movement, and gym. Music and movement encouraged free expression, but most pupils of the day can only remember being asked to pretend that they were a tree swaying in the wind. Gym involved vaulting and climbing over a mini assault course. This was a hangover from military training during the war and was performed in underwear. Eleven was a crucial age for children as they had to sit the Eleven-plus exam. Very often it would shape the rest of their lives. If you passed you went to a grammar school, failure would see you go to a secondary modern or technical college.

The Eleven-plus Exam

Background

After the Second World War, the state funded secondary education system was divided using a Tripartite system containing grammar schools, secondary technical colleges and secondary modern schools. The Eleven-plus examination was used to select which pupils went to which schools based on ability. As technical colleges were not available on the scale envisaged the exam came to symbolise fierce competition for places at the prestigious grammar schools. The very name still deeply divides opinion with many believing it was the symbol of a segregated two-tier school system whilst for others it set the educational benchmark.

Here's your chance to test yourself with example questions from the 1950s:
(Answers on page 96)

Arithmetic Questions

Question One: A motorist who left home at 11.15am, drives at 36 miles per hour. He stops for lunch from 1.15pm to 2.45pm and then continues his journey at 40 miles per hour. How many miles in total has he travelled by 6pm?

Question Two: 785 is multiplied by 50 and the result is divided by 125. Write down the answer.

Question Three: A ship uses 200 gallons of diesel for a voyage of 300 miles. How far could it travel using 80 gallons?

Question Four: Write in figures the sum of three hundred and seventy six and eighty-nine.

Question Five: Elizabeth is 8 years old and her father is 38. Answer the following:

A) How old was Elizabeth's father when he was 6 times as old as her?

B) In how many years' time will her father be three times as old as Elizabeth?

C) How old will Elizabeth be when her father becomes 15 times as old as she was 4 years ago?

General Intelligence Questions

Question One: Each of the following jumbled sentences can make sense by interchanging two words. Rewrite the sentences:

A) A was stung by Billy bee.

B) The shepherd whistled by the gate and stood to his dog.

C) The swim went to the pool for a family.

Question Two: The letters PELAP are the letters of the word APPLE jumbled up. Rearrange the following:

A) TOUNOCC is a fruit which comes from abroad.

B) FARFIGE is a large animal.

C) TIPACRAI is a girl's name.

Question Three: Each of the following sentences contains one error. Rewrite the sentences correctly:

A) When the dog saw me, it wagged it's tail.

B) The subject doesn't concern you or I.

C) Whilst speaking to my brother, the police car past me.

Top 10 Girls' Baby Names [1]

1. Susan	of Hebrew origin meaning "Lily Rose"
2. Linda	from the German for *lime tree* via Spanish where it meant "Pretty"
3. Christine	of Latin and French origin meaning "Follower of Christ"
4. Margaret	from *Margarita*, the Old Persian name meaning "Pearl"
5. Janet	of Old English origin meaning "God's gracious gift"
6. Patricia	derived from the Latin word *Patrician* meaning "Noble"
7. Carol	originally an Old German man's name meaning "Freeman"
8. Elizabeth	of Hebrew origin meaning "God is my oath"
9. Mary	from Latin meaning "Star of the sea"
10. Anne	of Hebrew origin meaning "The gracious one"

Top 10 Boys' Baby Names [2]

1. David	corruption of the Hebrew name *Dawid* meaning "beloved"
2. John	of Hebrew origin meaning "God is Gracious"
3. Stephen	of Greek origin meaning "Garland or crown"
4. Michael	of Hebrew origin meaning "One who is like God"
5. Peter	of Greek and biblical origin meaning "Rock"
6. Robert	from Old German meaning "Bright Fame"
7. Paul	from Latin meaning "Small" or "Humble"
8. Alan	from the Celtic for "Harmony" or "Noble"
9. Christopher	of Greek origin meaning "Bearer of Christ"
10. Richard	from Old German meaning "Powerful leader"

[1 2] Data compiled by the Office for National Statistics 1954

5th February 1953 | A Sweet Day For Children

Children all over Great Britain were seen emptying out their piggy-banks and heading straight for the nearest sweet shop as the first unrationed sweets went on sale. Toffee apples were the biggest sellers, with sticks of nougat and liquorice strips also disappearing fast. Adults joined in the sugar frenzy, with men in the City queuing up in their lunch breaks to buy boiled sweets and to enjoy the luxury of being able to buy 2lb boxes of chocolates to take home for the weekend. The government and manufacturers were quick to reassure the public that there would be no repeat of the first attempt to de-ration sweets, in April 1949, when demand far outstripped supply and they were put back on ration after just four months. Sugar itself, though still remained rationed, and manufacturers said the Ministry of Food should have freed sugar supplies as well as those of sweets and chocolate. As it was they had to make enough sweets to meet the demand of a de-rationed market, but with only 54% of the sugar supplies they had before the war. Overall the industry gave a warm welcome to the news. "We are very glad about it," said a spokesman for the Cocoa, Chocolate and Confectionery Alliance "We will do all we can to make it work." Spending on sweets and chocolate jumped by about £100m in the first year to £250m - a year which, according to the confectionery industry, was "as dynamic as any in the industry's history".

At the start of 1953 certain foods were still being rationed following the war so the evening meal would often be a simple affair. Sugar, for example, was still rationed until later in the year. Meat rationing ended in 1954. Refrigeration was still a luxury most could not afford so food would often be bought daily.

Pictured is Margaret Jones at her home in North Wales. She is collecting a plate of homemade butter from the scullery ready for the evening meal.

Mr. Davidson is seen writing a letter to his sister who lives in the United States. Writing bureaus were sought after pieces of furniture in the 1950s, often being passed down the generations as family heirlooms.

Relaxing in their armchairs in the front room of their house are teachers Mr. and Mrs. Samuel from Ebbw Vale. To the right is the tiled fireplace, a focal point for the family to gather around. The hearth is also a particular favourite for the family cat, Shan.

Dick Parry, toymaker, shows some of his Christmas toys to his children at the family home in Shrewsbury. Toy trains and doll houses featured heavily on the Christmas lists of fifties children.

Lucienne Day, pictured here, with her Calyx fabric pattern. This design generated a new school of pattern-making which became known as the 'Contemporary' style.

The Birth of Modern Design

By the 1950s Britain was slowly emerging from the privations of the Great Depression of the 1930s and from the 1940s which were overshadowed by war and its resultant shortages. The 1950s slowly became the age of the consumer and in the home it was very much "out with the old and in with the new." The 1950s was also an age when the political parties competed with each other to build new public housing. The Prime Minister Winston Churchill summoned the Housing Minister, Harold Macmillan, and tasked him with matching the previous Labour Government's achievement of building 200,000 new homes each year. These houses were smaller than pre-war homes, so furniture had to stack or be light enough to move around. Earlier inventions like serving trolleys, collapsible ironing boards and sofa beds became more commonplace. Nowhere could change be better seen than in the kitchen. Cottage style kitchens were replaced with sleek new fitted kitchens and for many the pantry was replaced by a refrigerator for the first time.

The 1950s were also a time of great design and the most enduring furniture was created by the husband and wife team of Charles and Ray Eames who produced stylish plywood, plastic and leather furniture. Another husband and wife team who brought elegance and colour into the home were Robin and Lucienne Day. Lucienne was the most influential British textile designer of the age. Her most famous design, Calyx, was created as a furnishing fabric and was used on the furniture designed by her husband. It was an abstract pattern composed of cup-shaped motifs joined by spindly lines and is one of the most recognisable and iconic designs of the 1950s.

Coronation Chicken

Coronation Chicken was a dish created to mark the coronation of Queen Elizabeth II in 1953. It was a variation of Jubilee Chicken, which was created for the Silver Jubilee of George V in 1935. The dish consists of cold cooked chicken, which is usually poached, combined with a creamy mayonnaise-based sauce that contains Indian spices, such as curry powder, and dried fruit like raisins. It is typically served as a sandwich filling, salad ingredient, or as part of a cold buffet. The dish was created by Constance Spry, an English food writer and Rosemary Hume, a chef and was originally served at the reception following the coronation ceremony. The dish was intended to showcase the best of British cuisine, while also incorporating elements of Indian cuisine, which was fashionable at the time due to the British Empire's long history with India. The dish quickly gained popularity, becoming a staple of British cuisine, appearing in many cookbooks and restaurants. It is still very popular today and is often served at picnics, buffets and other casual gatherings.

A recipe for classic Coronation Chicken from 1953 (Serves 6)

Ingredients

- 1 medium sized chicken (around 4lbs)
- 1 pint and a half chicken stock (or enough to cover the chicken)
- 1 onion, chopped
- 1 bay leaf
- 3 teaspoons curry powder
- 6oz mayonnaise
- 2oz plain yogurt (or 8oz of mayonnaise if yoghurt is unavailable)
- 2 tablespoons apricot jam (or mango chutney if available)
- 2 tablespoons lemon juice
- 3 oz cup raisins
- Salt and pepper, to taste

Method: Poach the chicken in the chicken stock with the onion and bay leaf until cooked through, about 60-80 mins. Remove from heat and let cool. In a small bowl, mix together the curry powder, mayonnaise, yogurt, apricot jam or mango chutney, lemon juice and raisins. Skin and bone the chicken and cut into bite-sized pieces and mix with the sauce. Season with salt and pepper. Chill in the refrigerator until ready to serve. Serve over a bed of greens or as a sandwich filling. Garnish with chopped parsley, if desired. **Enjoy!**

Pineapple Upside-Down Cake

Puddings were an essential part of dinner time in 1950s Britain, with some remembered more fondly than others. Jam roly-poly, tapioca, semolina, rice pudding, stewed fruit and custard or just plain old jelly and ice cream; all could follow the main meal. For something fancier, perhaps when having guests or family to dinner, a pineapple upside down cake made for a spectacular centrepiece. Tinned pineapples rings were relatively cheap and the number used was governed by the number in the tin. Small tins had 4 rings, large tins 7 or 8.

Recipe (Serves 8)

Ingredients

For the cake:
7 pineapple rings (tinned)
7 glacé cherries
4oz softened butter
4oz caster or demerara sugar
2 large eggs or 3 small ones
4oz self raising flour
¼ teaspoon vanilla extract (optional)

For the sauce:
2oz butter, plus extra for greasing
3oz caster or demerara sugar

Method: Preheat the oven to gas mark 4/ 350 F. Lightly grease the baking tin. Melt 2oz butter and 3oz sugar in a pan and stir until combined. Pour the mixture into the tin, then arrange the pineapple rings on top, popping a cherry into the centre of each ring. Beat the remaining butter and sugar together until light and fluffy. Then beat in the eggs one at a time, beating well with each addition. Add a tablespoon of flour with the second egg (or third one if you are using small ones). Beat in the vanilla extract (if using) then fold in the remaining flour. Spoon the mixture carefully into the cake tin and spread evenly over the pineapple and cherries. Bake in the centre of the oven for 35 minutes or until the cake is springy to the touch Allow the cake to cool in the tin for five minutes before turning out onto a plate. Serve warm with cream, ice cream or custard. **Delicious!**

Although introduced in the mid-1940s, the modern bikini was still very controversial and met with considerable social resistance. However in the early 1950s stars such as Brigitte Bardot played a large part in bringing the bikini into the mainstream.

Undaunted by the situation these pocket-sized models are demonstrating the latest look for children at a fashion show.

Ladies wearing lavish ball gowns, two with intricate embroidered floral patterns.

This elegant dress is set off with a fitted black waist belt and matching shoes.

Fashion in 1953

Three types of beach/ nautical themed summer dresses. Geometric patterns would became a 1950s design hallmark.

On location in Switzerland, film star Audrey Hepburn is pictured wearing a popular linen dress style with the fashionable tight fitting waist belt.

The 1950's saw the rise of the sports jacket or sports coat for men. These patterned jackets were designed to be worn without matching trousers. Corduroy, suede, leather, denim and tweed were popular fabrics.

Father and son modelling formal coats for the winter. Trousers were loose fitting whilst Homburg hats remained popular.

The Great British Seaside Holiday

Thanks to the Holiday With Pay Act of 1938, Britons were allowed an annual paid holiday, although this gave them a measly week off per year. In 1953 those working in factories would often all have to take their holidays at the same time as production was halted in the summer. Better employers gave their workers two weeks. Only one in fifteen people ventured abroad, as few had the means to afford foreign travel. Popular destinations were those that could be reached by ferry such as France, Ireland, Holland and Belgium, although visitors to Ireland were swollen by the Irish population in Britain going home to visit family.

Relaxing by the swimming pool

A day trip to the seaside was very popular

Italy was a popular longer haul destination, but this would normally involve a flight, which would double the cost of the holiday. So for most a holiday meant one thing, a train journey to the Great British seaside, which was in its heyday. There were three main options as to where to stay. First, the guest house, with its list of rules about breakfast time and when you could use your room. Secondly, there were many holiday camps, some of which occupied old army barracks left over from the war. Camps such as Butlin's offered entertainment for both children and adults.

There was sandcastle building and sports and games such as tug-of-war and the three-legged races for the children. For adults there were sports and dancing. There were also competitions for the adults, including Miss Lovely Legs and Mr Knobbly Knees. The third and most cost-effective option was to stay with a relative, usually an older family member, who had retired to live by the coast. Much time was spent on the beach, if the weather allowed. In the 1950s people did not think of using sunblock and the aim was to get as tanned as possible as fast as possible.

Messing around in the diving competition

A bucket and spade holiday

Very often tanning accelerators were used and were homemade concoctions. One such potion was created by mixing vegetable oils with puréed carrots. In order to get and show off your tan, bathing costumes were needed. Women were increasingly sporting a bikini, a two-piece swimsuit which had been designed by the Parisian fashion house of Jacques Heim. Men would sport shorts or trunks. Many children of the era have strong memories of wearing knitted woollen costumes, often created by a generous auntie. This would act like a sponge when the children entered the water and then get filled with sand on the beach. Upon drying they would then take on the composition of cement and become extremely uncomfortable.

Father Christmas arrives by train to hand out presents to an awaiting gathering of families

Two excited children opening their presents with their mother and grandfather watching over

Christmas and Hogmanay 1953

In Scotland the celebration of Christmas was muted in the 1950s. A dispute between the Calvinist Church of Scotland and the Catholic Church of Rome saw Christmas celebrations effectively banned for 400 years. Shops were not decorated and even Christmas trees and decorations in the home were few and far between. The fact that Christmas Day did not become a public holiday until 1958, meant the day was much like any other in Scotland. The Scots instead saved all their revelry for New Year – Hogmanay. There were several traditions and superstitions that had to be taken care of before midnight. The house had to be cleaned and ashes from the fire taken out on New Years Eve. At the stroke of midnight someone, usually a dark haired man, would bring coal, shortbread and possibly a wee dram of whisky into the house, in a tradition known as first-footing. Then the party would well and truly begin with a rendition of Robert Burns' *Auld Lang Syne*. South of the border Christmas was celebrated with more gusto. Houses were adorned with trees and paper- chains, which were often homemade. Cards from relatives, neighbours and friends would be hung on string. Many would contain letters and might be the only written communication all year.

The celebrations in 1953 were particularly special as Christmas Day fell on a Friday, meaning that the combined holiday of that and Boxing Day gave those who did not work at weekends a four day break. Christmas Eve was a time of particular excitement for children. They were encouraged to go to their beds by the promise of a visit from Father Christmas, and a mince pie and an alcoholic beverage were put out for him in preparation for his arrival. Many over-excited children slept with one eye open and noticed that Father Christmas bore more than a passing resemblance to their own father. They would wake up in the morning to the sight of a Christmas stocking or a pillow case, which contained assorted presents and the ubiquitous satsuma. As with today the Christmas dinner took centre stage. Turkey had not yet become the meat of choice and chicken was too expensive. Instead beef was a staple for most. Britain was still in a time of austerity and many people grew their own vegetables, so the trimmings were abundant and of high nutritional value. The dinner was usually timed to finish before or start after the Queen's Speech. This was her first Christmas speech since her coronation. Her pre-recorded broadcast (given during a visit to New Zealand) was heard on radio only at 3pm (it was first televised in 1957) and families would gather round and listen in silence to Her Majesty.

The 1953 Oscars, the 25th Academy Awards, were held on 19th March 1953 at the RKO Pantages Theatre in Hollywood, California and the NBC National Theatre in New York to honour the best films of 1952. The ceremonies were broadcast live on NBC hosted by Bob Hope on the west coast and Fredric March on the east. The big winner of the night was the film *The Greatest Show on Earth*, directed by Cecil B. DeMille, which won Best Picture and Best Motion Picture Story. Other notable winners included Gary Cooper, who won Best Actor for his role in *High Noon* and Shirley Booth, who won Best Actress for her role in *Come Back, Little Sheba*. The award for Best Supporting Actor went to Anthony Quinn for his role in *Viva Zapata!* with the award for Best Supporting Actress going to Gloria Grahame for her part in *The Bad and the Beautiful*. The film *The Quiet Man*, directed by John Ford and starring John Wayne and Maureen O'Hara, won the award for Best Director. The British music scene in 1953 was still recovering from the aftermath of World War II. The popular music of the time was dominated by traditional jazz and dance bands, with popular acts including Acker Bilk, Chris Barber and Ken Colyer. Skiffle, a style of folk music with jazz and blues influences, was also emerging as a popular genre led by Lonnie Donegan. In the early 1950s, American rock and roll began to make an impact in the UK, with the Bill Haley & His Comets' hit *Rock Around the Clock* reaching the top of the charts in 1955. This marked the beginning of the rock and roll era in the UK, which would eventually lead to the British Invasion of the USA in the 1960s. The BBC played an important role in the British music scene at the time, with its Light Programme radio station featuring popular music programmes such as *Housewives' Choice* and *Two-Way Family Favourites*. The BBC also held an annual *Light Programme Dance Band Contest*, which helped to promote emerging acts. Overall, the British music scene in 1953 was a mix of traditional jazz, dance bands and emerging styles such as skiffle foreshadowing the cultural revolution that was to come in the following decades. In 1953, theatre played a significant role in entertainment, culture and social commentary. Broadway was the epicentre of American theatre, and productions ranged from musicals to dramas. Some of the notable productions that premiered included *The Crucible* by Arthur Miller, *Can-Can* by Cole Porter and *The Caine Mutiny Court-Martial* by Herman Wouk. These plays dealt with important themes such as political persecution, censorship and military justice. However, the 1950s was also a time of conservative social values and anti-communist paranoia. The House Un-American Activities Committee (HUAC) investigated alleged communist influence in the entertainment industry, leading to the blacklisting of several artists and writers. The impact of the HUAC's investigations was felt in the movie world as well, with several writers and actors being targeted and scrutinised including Charlie Chaplin, Orson Welles and Leonard Bernstein.

Cecil B. DeMille

John Wayne and Maureen O'Hara

Calamity Jane

Doris Day

Starring Doris Day and Howard Keel
Directed by David Butler
Released on 4th November 1953

The film is loosely based on the life of Martha Jane Cannary, also known as Calamity Jane, a frontierswoman who became famous for her exploits in the American Wild West. Set in the late 19th century, it follows Calamity Jane, a tomboyish and rough-around-the-edges woman, who works as a scout for the U.S. Army at Fort Scully in Deadwood, South Dakota. Calamity develops a rivalry with Wild Bill Hickok (played by Howard Keel), a famous gunslinger who comes to town. She also befriends Katie Brown (played by Allyn McLerie), an actress from Chicago who has come to perform in Deadwood. The movie features a number of musical numbers, including the song *Secret Love*, which won an Academy Award for Best Original Song. Other notable songs include *The Black Hills of Dakota* and *Just Blew in from the Windy City*. While the film takes some liberties with the real-life story of Calamity Jane, it captures the spirit of the Wild West and the pioneering women who helped settle the frontier. Doris Day gives a memorable performance as the tough and independent Calamity, and the film remains a beloved classic to this day. Eagle-eyed movie-goers noticed that the western street exteriors portrayed as Deadwood City had earlier been used as war-torn Atlanta in *Gone with the Wind*, as well as appearing in countless Warner Brothers westerns.

From Here to Eternity

Starring Burt Lancaster, Montgomery Clift, Deborah Kerr, Frank Sinatra and Donna Reed
Directed by Fred Zinnemann. Released on 5th August 1953

From Here to Eternity is based on a 1951 book of the same name. At the time of the original novel's release, it was dubbed "From Here to Obscenity" because of its frank content and profane language. The book was banned in libraries across the US for years. The film is set in the months before the attack on Pearl Harbor and follows a group of US soldiers stationed in Hawaii in 1941. It centres on the relationships between the soldiers and the difficulties they face in their personal and professional lives, including love triangles and conflict with superiors. It won eight Academy Awards, including Best Picture, Best Supporting Actor (Sinatra) and Best Supporting Actress (Reed). It is widely regarded as a classic of war cinema and is remembered for its powerful performances, stunning cinematography and timeless themes of love and sacrifice. It is known for its iconic beach scene between Lancaster and Kerr, which was highly controversial at the time due to its suggestive content (think waves crashing on a beach). It was a huge box office success and helped to launch Sinatra's career as a dramatic actor. In addition, it was seen as a significant milestone in the representation of minorities in Hollywood, with the character of Private Maggio (played by Sinatra) being depicted as a multi-dimensional character with Italian-American heritage.

Gentlemen Prefer Blondes

Starring Jane Russell and Marilyn Monroe
Directed by Howard Hawks
Released on 1st July 1953

Anita Loos's famous novel and play *Gentlemen Prefer Blondes* was made into a musical and ran for 740 performances during the 1949-1951 season. It was the breakout role for Carol Channing in her career on Broadway. But for the screen version, a pair of pulchritudinous sex symbols were cast as the showgirls looking for husbands, namely Jane Russell and Marilyn Monroe playing Dorothy Shaw and Lorelei Lee respectively. Most of the Jule Styne/Leo Robin score from Broadway was scrapped. Two numbers written by Hoagy Carmichael and Harold Adamson were added. Retained from the original score was *Bye Bye Baby*, *Two Little Girls from Little Rock* and the famous golddiggers' theme, *Diamonds are a Girl's Best Friend*. The story was also updated from when it was originally written during the Roaring Twenties to the current Fifties. However, the motivations of the two leading characters remained the same. Both would like to find husbands. Dorothy Lee (Russell) wants to marry for love with money being a bonus, but for Lorelei Lee (Monroe) it's strictly mercenary. The two men they are pursuing are millionaire's son Gus Esmond Jr. (Tommy Noonan) for Lorelei whilst Dorothy has her eye on Ernie Malone (Elliott Reid). Monroe's mercenary ways nearly sink the two of them, but it all kind of works out in the end.

Marilyn Monroe

How to Marry a Millionaire

Starring Marilyn Monroe, Betty Grable, and Lauren Bacall
Directed by Jean Negulesco
Released on 5th November 1953

The film is a romantic comedy that follows the lives of three women, Schatze, Loco and Pola, who rent a luxurious apartment in New York City with the sole intention of attracting and marrying wealthy men. Schatze (Bacall) is a former model who is looking for a rich husband to support her lavish lifestyle. Loco (Grable) is a sophisticated woman who is tired of dating men who cannot provide for her, while Pola (Monroe) is a ditzy but lovable woman who wants to find a man who will take care of her. Throughout the film, the three women navigate the challenges of finding suitable partners, including dealing with pretentious and manipulative men; all the while trying to maintain their true personalities while also attempting to appeal to the rich and wealthy. However, as they go through their journey, they learn important lessons about love, friendship and what truly matters in life. In a fact meets fiction moment, Lauren Bacall's character Shatze says "I've always liked older men ....Look at that old fellow, what's his name, in the African Queen; absolutely crazy about him." She is referring to her real-life husband Humphrey Bogart. *How to Marry a Millionaire* was a commercial success, grossing over $5 million at the box office and was widely acclaimed for its witty script, comedic timing and the chemistry between the three leading actresses.

I Confess

Starring Montgomery Clift, Anne Baxter and Karl Malden
Directed by Alfred Hitchcock
Released on 12th February 1953

I Confess is a classic film directed by the legendary filmmaker Alfred Hitchcock. A Catholic priest named Father Michael Logan becomes embroiled in a murder case. The plot revolves around a revelation made by a murderer to Father Logan in the confessional. This leads to the priest being the prime suspect in the murder investigation. Despite being innocent, Father Logan is unable to reveal what he heard, as such things are protected by the seal of the confessional. The movie follows the priest as he tries to clear his name while struggling with his own conscience and the vows he has taken as a priest. It is a well-crafted mystery thriller with suspenseful scenes, tense moments and a thought-provoking plot. The film showcases Hitchcock's trademark style, including his use of music, lighting and camera techniques, to create a sense of unease and keep the audience engaged. The film's themes of guilt, sin and moral dilemma add depth to the story. It also features standout performances by its lead actors, particularly Montgomery Clift who delivers a nuanced and powerful portrayal of a man caught between his duty to the church and his desire to clear his name. The movie was banned in Ireland because it showed a priest having a relationship with a woman, even though the relationship took place before the character became a priest.

Richard Burton

The Robe

Starring Richard Burton, Jean Simmons and Victor Mature
Directed by Henry Koster
Released on 16th September 1953

The Robe is based on the novel of the same name by Lloyd C. Douglas. The story follows Marcellus Gallio (Richard Burton), a Roman tribune who is in charge of the crucifixion of Jesus Christ. After winning Christ's robe in a game of dice, Marcellus starts to have strange dreams and experiences that lead him on a journey of self-discovery and ultimately conversion to Christianity. Marcellus struggles to reconcile his new faith with his duties as a Roman soldier, but with the help of his slave Demetrius (Victor Mature) and the love of Diana (Jean Simmons), he finds the strength to stand up for his beliefs. The film was notable for being the first motion picture to be released in the widescreen format CinemaScope, which gave audiences a more immersive viewing experience. It was also praised for its impressive sets and costumes, as well as the performances of its lead actors. *The Robe* was a commercial success, earning over $17 million at the box office and winning two Academy Awards for Best Art Direction and Best Costume Design, The film's popularity also led to a sequel, *Demetrius and the Gladiators*, which was released in 1954. That film also starred Victor Mature and featured a young Anne Bancroft.

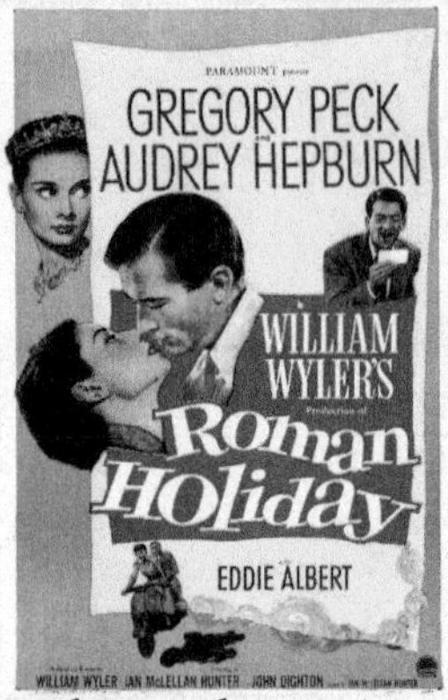

Roman Holiday

Starring Audrey Hepburn and Gregory Peck
Directed by William Wyler
Released on 27th August 1953

The film is a romantic comedy set in Rome and follows the story of a young princess, Ann, who is tired of her monotonous life and duties. One day, she decides to escape her handlers and experience the city on her own. She meets an American journalist named Joe Bradley (Peck), who initially sees her as a story to report on. However, as they spend time together, he finds himself torn between his duty as a journalist and his growing affection for Ann. Audrey Hepburn shines in her role as Ann, conveying the character's restless spirit and longing for a sense of freedom. The film showcases the beauty of Rome and its historical landmarks including the Colosseum, the Spanish Steps and the Trevi Fountain, making it a delightful travelogue for audiences. The film received critical acclaim upon release and is still considered a classic of its genre. Hepburn was awarded an Academy Award for Best Actress for her performance and the film was nominated for several other awards. The film's memorable soundtrack, composed by Georges Auric, includes the song *Three Coins in the Fountain* which became a hit. This was the first American movie to be shot entirely in Italy. Director William Wyler had good reason to remove himself from the US as he was being investigated by the House Un-American Activities Committee for his liberal views.

Shane

Starring Alan Ladd, Jean Arthur and Jack Palance
Directed by George Stevens
Released on 23rd April 1953

The film is set in the late 1800s and follows a retired gunslinger named Shane (Ladd), who comes to a Wyoming homestead and gets caught up in a conflict between settlers and cattlemen. Shane's calm demeanour and quick-draw skills make him a natural defender of the settlers. He soon finds himself drawn into a dangerous struggle for power and control. The film is known for its stunning cinematography and memorable performances. In particular, Alan Ladd as Shane and Jean Arthur who plays a settler's wife, Marian Starrett shine. Jack Palance also delivers a standout performance as the ruthless cattle baron, Jack Wilson. *Shane* is one of the best Western films ever made and has been praised for its timeless themes of violence, courage and the struggle for justice. The film explores the idea of the "gunfighter myth" and the complex moral dilemmas faced by those who live and work on the frontier. It's also notable for its portrayal of the relationship between Shane and a young boy, Joey, who idolises him. The film also perfectly captures the loneliness and isolation of life on the frontier. Clint Eastwood has stated that *Shane* was a huge influence on his acting and directorial career. Its atmospheric style has been copied many times since. Billy Crystal has stated that the performance of Brandon de Wilde, as Joey, inspired him to take up acting.

Tokyo Story

Starring Setsuko Hara and Chishū Ryū
Directed by Yasujirō Ozu
Released on 3rd November 1953

This film is widely considered as a masterpiece of Japanese cinema, and is cited as one of the greatest films of all time. It follows an aged couple who travel from their rural home to Tokyo to visit their children, but find themselves largely ignored and marginalised by them. The film explores themes of ageing, family relationships and the changing society in post-war Japan. Shot in Ozu's signature style, it features long takes and a fixed camera position. The slow pace and lack of action, combined with deep emotional resonance, make it a unique and memorable experience. Its use of subtlety and understated emotion, combined with its poignant portrayal of family dynamics, has earned it critical acclaim and a cult following. Despite its humble subject matter, *Tokyo Story* is a powerful meditation on the complexities of family relationships and the shifting values of a rapidly changing society. Its exploration of the disconnection between generations and the distance that can grow between family members is a universal theme that still resonates today. The film remains a touchstone of Japanese cinema and continues to be celebrated for Ozu's masterful storytelling. Charles Micherer of Newsweek said it was "like a Japanese paper flower that is dropped into water and then swells to fill the entire container with its beauty."

House of Wax

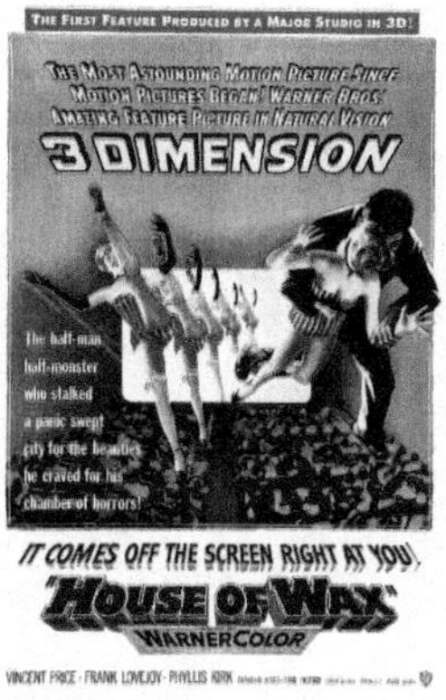

Starring Vincent Price, Frank Lovejoy, Phyllis Kirk and Charles Bronson
Directed by Andre De Toth
Released on 10th April 1953

House of Wax was the first film to be released in 3D with stereophonic sound. In it, Professor Henry Jarrod (Vincent Price) is a true artist whose wax sculptures are lifelike. He specialises in historical tableaux such as Marie Antoinette and Joan of Arc. His business partner, Matthew Burke (Roy Roberts), needs some of his investment returned to him and pushes Jarrod to have more lurid exposés like a chamber of horrors. When Jarrod refuses, Burke set the place alight destroying all of his beautiful work in the hope of claiming the insurance. Jarrod is believed to have died in the fire, but he unexpectedly reappears some 18 months later when he opens a new exhibit. This time, his displays focus on the macabre but he has yet to reproduce his most cherished work, Marie Antoinette. When he meets his new assistant's beautiful friend, Sue Allen (Phyllis Kirk), he knows he's found the perfect model. However, unbeknownst to anyone, he has a very particular way of making his wax creations. Sue makes a shocking discovery in the finale and faces mortal danger from Jarrod and his deaf and mute sidekick, Igor (an early performance from the actor Charles Bronson). The film has something of a "B" movie feel about it and over the years it has been enjoyed more for its poor special effects and comedic script, rather than its shock value.

Fewer than two million British homes owned a TV set at the beginning of 1953. These were mainly in London, Manchester, Birmingham, Cardiff and Glasgow. But in the build-up to the coronation, over half a million sets were sold or rented as royal fever swept the nation. However, those who owned a TV were still very much in the minority. Radio still provided news and entertainment for the majority of the nation. The most notable radio debut came in the form of *The Glums*, a comedy about a dysfunctional family, written by Frank Muir and Denis Norden. Some programmes such as *Workers' Playtime*, which began during WW2, were still running from 'A factory somewhere in England'. A few performers of that time would turn up at a factory canteen and perform live to the workers. Singers were accompanied by piano only and would perform in between comedy acts by the likes of Arthur Askey, Tommy Trinder and Ted Ray. All were masters of their craft. Morning Radio was heavily slanted towards wives and mothers as career women were almost unheard of. Programmes included *Housewives' Choice*, *Music While You Work* and *Mrs. Dale's Diary* (an early soap opera). Afternoon radio was more relaxing and there would be a lunchtime light drama almost every day. This was seen as a time for the hardworking housewife to put her feet up before the children came home from school and then her husband from work. Band Shows were still thriving at the weekend, with Billy Cotton and Victor Sylvester leading the way. There was also *In Town Tonight* which was a national institution from 1933 to 1960. It was an early form of chat show which included reviews and celebrity gossip, but tame by today's standards. Radio also played a big part in children's lives. At school they could listen to educational programmes such as *Nature Study*, aimed at 9 to 11 year-olds, which ran from 1927 to 1965. Older children could learn languages via programmes like *Early Stages in French*, which was broadcast between 1952 and 1965. Pre-school children were treated to *Listen with Mother*, which could easily have been titled *Sit Still, Mother Has Something Better To Do*! It filled a slot in the middle of the afternoon at a quarter to two. The format entailed a short story, some nursery rhymes and a sing-along. All services were provided by the BBC, the only sanctioned broadcaster of the day.

Tommy Trinder (with Jean Colin)

Desmond Carrington, a presenter of Housewives' Choice

Children gathering around the radio

Watch With Mother

Ran from 1952 to 1980

Compered by Dom Gemmel (first 2 shows) then Leonard Sachs

Andy Pandy

Watch With Mother, a general title for a series of five individual programmes, was the first planned combination of entertainment and education on British television. It was specifically designed for very small children with each day having its own particular theme. Along with BBC radio's *Listen with Mother*, which began in 1950, it represented a shift in BBC policy to make programmes for this very young audience both on radio and television. *Picture Book* was the first segment produced. It screened on Mondays featuring Bizzy Lizzy and Sausage the Dachshund. *Andy Pandy* was shown on Tuesday. *Bill and Ben (The Flowerpot Men)* was shown on Wednesday. A story about a hedgehog, a mouse and a rabbit called *Rag, Tag and Bobtail* aired in the Thursday slot whilst Friday saw *The Woodentops*. The show was much beloved by children and parents alike with each episode being eagerly anticipated. When the BBC dropped *Watch With Mother* temporarily to show the cricket, thousands of letters reached the Corporation from mothers complaining that their children had been left in tears. The BBC had to promise it would not happen again. In the 1960s and 1970s, a new stream of programmes was created for the series. *Pogle's Wood*, *Trumpton*, *Tales of the Riverbank*, *The Herbs* and *Mary, Mungo and Midge* all saw their debuts. Later still came 'changing room explorer' *Mr. Benn*, 'loose at the seams' *Bagpuss*, *Fingerbobs* and *Bod*.

All Your Own

Ran from 1952 to 1961

Presented by Huw Wheldon, Olive Shapley and Cliff Michelmore

Olive Shapley (right)

Introduced by Huw Wheldon (later to become BBC Director of Television) alongside Olive Shapley (of radio's Woman's Hour) and frequently produced by a young Cliff Michelmore, *All Your Own* gave children the opportunity to display their own individual skills and talents or discuss their hobbies and pastimes. The show guided a young guitarist by the name of John Williams on his first step to stardom, and it did the same for The King Brothers, a popular middle-of-the-road group from the 1960s. Future Led Zeppelin guitar maestro Jimmy Page was also a youthful guest. One guest who did not however enjoy a fruitful, or indeed lengthy career was a pet mouse brought along by a schoolboy in company with the lad's other pet, an eagle. While Wheldon was enthusing about how amazing it was that in the wild the mouse would be the eagle's natural prey yet in captivity they seemed the best of friends, the eagle let his instincts get the better of him and suddenly swooped from his perch and ate the mouse. Wheldon also once casually leant on a harpsichord made entirely out of matchsticks by a child and reduced it to ruins. He commented, "I'm sure you can stick it back together again." Ah, well that's show business! It all makes *Blue Peter's* incident with the elephant seem tame in comparison. Very little footage of the programme has survived, a bit like the mouse.

I Love Lucy

Ran from October 15th 1951 to May 6th 1957
Starring Lucille Ball, Desi Arnaz, Vivian Vance and William Frawley

I Love Lucy was an American television sitcom that originally aired from 1951 to 1957. The show was created by Lucille Ball and her husband Desi Arnaz. It was one of the first sitcoms to be shot on 35mm film in front of a live audience. It centred around the antics of Lucy Ricardo, a housewife living in New York City, with her bandleader husband Ricky Ricardo. Lucy is often scheming and getting into comical situations, much to the delight of audiences. The show was also known for its diverse cast, including Cuban-American actor Desi Arnaz and African-American actress Vivian Vance. *I Love Lucy* was a huge success and remains one of the most popular TV shows of all time. It won numerous awards and was beloved for its humour and the chemistry between its lead actors. The show was innovative for its use of multiple cameras, which allowed for more complex shots and greater freedom in editing. The theme song *I Love Lucy* became iconic and is still recognised today. Fact met fiction in the episode *Lucy Goes to the Hospital*, which aired on 19th January 1953. In it, Lucy gives birth. 24hrs before the show was screened she gave birth in real life to Desi Arnaz Jr. 73.9% of all American homes with television sets tuned in, amounting to 44 million viewers watching the episode. This was a record until 9th September 1956, when Elvis Presley appeared for the first time on *The Ed Sullivan Show*, which drew an audience share of 82.6%.

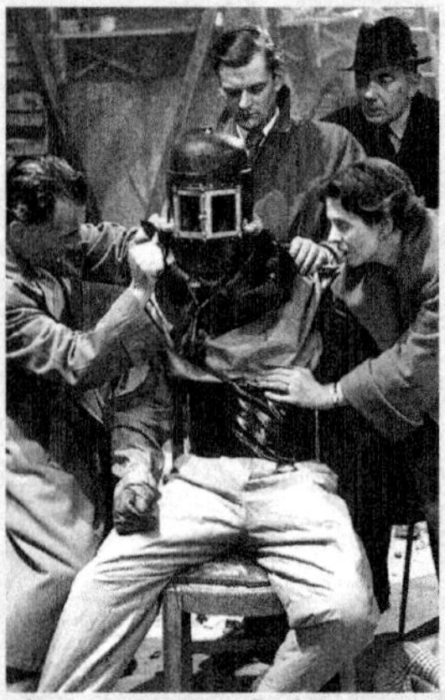

The Quatermass Experiment

Ran from July 18th to August 22nd 1953 (Six episodes)
Starring Reginald Tate, Isabel Dean and Hugh Kelly

Professor Bernard Quatermass, Director General of the British Experimental Rocket Group, launches the first manned space flight from Australia. A malfunction sends the rocket and its three man crew thousands of miles off course. When the rocket returns to Earth, it crashes in Wimbledon. To the shock of Quatermass, his team and the spectators who gather around the crash site, only one of the three crewmen, Victor Carroon, is still aboard. Carroon seems unwell, barely able to talk. Examinations of the rocket by both Quatermass and Scotland Yard's Inspector Lomax reveal that something attacked the crew of the rocket as they were on course back to Earth. Even more alarming is that Carroon seems to be undergoing some sort of metamorphosis, which is accelerated by a botched kidnapping attempt by foreign agents. Although the special effects in the series are pretty rudimentary compared with today, the programme was still able to generate tension. It had many viewers, particularly the younger ones, watching from behind the sofa. The series was broadcast live and was not without its mishaps. In an unusual illustration of the problems encountered with early live broadcasts, the telerecording of the second episode *Persons Reported Missing* was partially obscured by an insect which landed on one of the cameras during the broadcast. Only two of the original episodes have survived on tape. There were three further *Quatermass* series.

Ken Dodd

The Good Old Days

Ran from 20th July 1953 to 31st December 1983

Compered by Dom Gemmel (first 2 shows) then Leonard Sachs

Early in 1953 producer Barney Colehan devised a one-off show entitled *The Story of the Music Hall* presented by Deryck Guyler. The programme proved so popular that it was decided to create a series under the title of *The Good Old Days*.The show was a re-creation of the Music Hall variety shows that were popular in the late Victorian and the Edwardian periods (late 1800s and early 1900s). Entertainers performed musical, comedy, magic and recitation acts on stage in Edwardian costume. In some cases acts would appear as famous Edwardian music hall performers such as Vesta Tilly. Even the audience was dressed in authentic costumes. The show always ended with the entire cast and the audience singing a rousing rendition of *Down at the Old Bull and Bush*. In the course of its run it featured about 2,000 performers. Whilst the pattern was unwavering, the performers themselves were many and varied, including Hattie Jaques, Les Dawson, Roy Hudd, Barbara Windsor, Danny La Rue, Frankie Vaughan, Larry Grayson, Ken Dodd, Roy Castle and Tommy Steele. However, the well-known faces were interspersed with unknown acts if they could perform in the traditional Music Hall style. Tap-dancing duos, comedy acrobatics and ventriloquy were popular. On 16th December 1983, *Goodbye to the Good Old Days* was shown, a documentary celebrating the end of the 30-year run. That year Barry Cryer served as narrator. The final show aired on New Year's Eve.

The Jack Benny Show

Ran from 1950 to 1965

Starring Jack Benny, Mary Livingstone, Eddie Anderson and Mel Blanc

Jack Benny played a character of the same name, a comedic version of himself as a penny-pinching, egotistical but lovable radio and later television personality. The show was a classic of the situation comedy genre, known for its strong ensemble cast, humorous storytelling and witty one-liners. One of the key elements of the show's humour was Benny's demeanour as a cheapskate, often quibbling over small amounts of money and frequently the butt of jokes about his advanced age. The show also featured a talented supporting cast, including Eddie Anderson as Benny's valet, Rochester; Mel Blanc (the voice of Bugs Bunny and Daffy Duck) as a variety of characters and Don Wilson as the announcer. In the *60-piece orchestra* skit aired on 25th January 1953, Jack explains to an interviewer in his dressing room that he would rather have been a concert violinist than a comedian. In a flash-back, we see him practising as a small boy. Jack imagines that he is playing with a large orchestra. Benny, who used to appear on stage threatening to play the violin, was actually a competent violinist. He was a friend of President Harry S. Truman and served as Master of Ceremonies for Truman's Inaugural Ball. When he arrived at the White House for the event, a guard pointed to his violin case and asked, "Mr. Benny, what do you have in there?" As a joke, Jack whispered back, "It's a Thompson sub-machine gun." The guard replied, "Oh, that's a relief. I was afraid it was your violin."

Jo Stafford

You Belong To Me

Performed by Jo Stafford

Written by Chilton Price (and possibly Redd Stewart and Pee Wee King)

Chilton Price was a music librarian at a radio station in Louisville, Kentucky. In her spare time she wrote songs which she would hand over to Stewart and Pee Wee. They would work on the arrangement and often revise the lyrics. The greatest song to emerge from this collaboration was *You Belong to Me*. The original version was recorded by Sue Thompson on Mercury's country label with another version, sung by Patti Page, making the top ten on the US Billboard Charts. By far the most successful cover was sung by Jo Stafford. Her version hit the American charts in August, and remained there for 24 weeks. In the UK, it later hit the number one spot making Stafford the first female artist to top the charts. Later, Chilton Price claimed that she should have had solo writing credits, but was pressured by Stewart and King to include them.

Frankie Laine

Answer Me

Performed by Frankie Laine, David Whitfield and others

Written by Carl Sigman

Answer Me is a popular song, originally written in 1952 (with German lyrics) under the title *Mütterlein*. The English lyrics were written by Carl Sigman. After the song was recorded by David Whitfield and Frankie Laine in 1953, the "religious" version was banned by the BBC after complaints. Nevertheless, it still reached number one on the UK Singles Chart, after another version was written by Sigman in which, in the new lyrics, "Answer me, Lord above..." is changed to "Answer me, oh my love..." with other appropriate changes. The new song, entitled *Answer Me, My Love*, was again recorded by Laine and Whitfield, but became a bigger US hit for Nat King Cole in 1954. Whitfield's version reached the top spot in the UK Singles Chart first, followed swiftly by Laine's. In December, for the only time in British chart history, the two versions of the same song were at number one together.

Charlie Chaplin

Eternally

Sung by Jimmy Young

Written by Charlie Chaplin

The song featured in the 1952 film *Limelight*, which Chaplin wrote, directed and starred in. In 1953 it was recorded by disc jockey, Jimmy Young who, unlike most DJs who tried their hand at recording, could actually sing. The song's melody is simple, but its lyrics express a deep longing for love and companionship that transcends time and space. It speaks of a love that lasts forever, even after death and celebrates the eternal bond between two souls. The song has been covered by numerous artists over the years, including Nat King Cole, Petula Clark, Vic Damone and Dinah Shore, but Chaplin's original version remains the most beloved with Jimmy Young's coming a close second. Young's version peaked at number 8 in the UK charts in September 1953. The message in the song is universal and a Spanish language version, titled *Candilejas (Footlights)*, topped the charts in Mexico in 1974.

Lita Roza

(How Much Is) That Doggie in the Window?

Sung in Great Britain by Lita Roza

Written by Bob Merill Released on 27th January 1953

When Lita Roza died in August 2008, her obituary in the Liverpool Daily Post recorded her thoughts on *That Doggie in the Window*: "It was rubbish, rubbish, rubbish!" After recording it, she never performed it again. Roza was so unhappy at having to record this that the heads of her record company felt compelled to make amends by sending a new vacuum cleaner to her house. Bad it may have been, but the song was a number one hit on both sides of the Atlantic; the original recording was by Oklahoma-born Patti Page. Her version with the Jack Rael Orchestra, and backed by My Jealous Eyes, was recorded on 18th December 1952, and topped the Billboard Chart. It was also recorded by Mandy Miller in 1953, and by Baby Jane & Rockabyes in 1963. After his death in 1998, Merill was rather unkindly branded "the worst songwriter of all time" by Slate magazine. That was more meow than woof woof!

Al Martino

Here in My Heart

Sung by Al Martino

Written by Pat Genaro, Lou Levinson and Bill Borrelli

Originally published on 1st May 1952

When Al Martino's friend and fellow crooner Mario Lanza decided not to record the song, it was both a blessing and a curse. It would give Martino a number one single on both sides of the Atlantic. It was the first official UK number one in the newly created New Musical Express charts. It cemented his place in the record books as well as being the answer in many a pub quiz. The bad luck was that his success brought the attention of the mafia who muscled in on his management team. The mob's threat was so potent that Martino feared for his life and would not return to America for seven years. The "B" side, *I Cried Myself to Sleep Last Night*, could not have been more appropriate.

Frankie Laine

I Believe

Performed by Frankie Laine

Written by Edwin Drake Released: 30th January 1953

"I believe for every drop of rain that falls, A flower grows, I believe that somewhere in the darkest night, A candle glows."

Frankie Laine said of the song: "It accomplished an awful lot in its day because it said all the things that need to be said in a prayer and yet it didn't use any of the holy words - Lord, God, Him, His, Thine, Thou. It said it all and it changed the whole spectrum of faith songs" Frankie Laine holds the record for most weeks at #1 for an artist in a single year: 27 weeks. His other hits *Hey Joe!* and *Answer Me* held the #1 spot for 2 and 7 weeks respectively and *I Believe* for 18 weeks. The song has been covered many times by artists such as Louis Armstrong, Barbra Streisand, Tom Jones and Elvis Presley.

I Saw Mommy Kissing Santa Claus

The Beverley Sisters

Originally performed by Jimmy Boyd

Written by Tommie Conner

I Saw Mommy Kissing Santa Claus is a popular Christmas song written and performed by Jimmy Boyd in 1952. It was recorded by Perry Como in 1953. The song is about a young boy who sees his mother kissing a man dressed in a Santa Claus costume and assumes that it must be the real Santa Claus. However, he later realises that it was just his father dressed up as Santa. The song has a light-hearted and playful tone, and its catchy melody has made it a holiday classic. It has been covered by many artists over the years including,The Ronettes, The Jackson 5 and a rather risqué version by Spike Jones. It remains a popular Christmas song to this day. The lyrics of the song evoke the joy and excitement of the holiday season and the magic of Christmas. A version of the song by The Beverley Sisters charted at number 6 in the UK in December 1953.

The Song from Moulin Rouge

Mantovani

Performed by Mantovani

Written by Georges Auric with lyrics by William Engvick

Mantovani was an Italian-born conductor and composer known for his lush orchestral arrangements of popular songs and light classical pieces. He became famous in the 1950s and 60s for his distinctive style, which utilised cascading strings and a heavy use of the harp, to create a distinctive "sweet" sound. He recorded over 100 albums and sold over 50 million records during his career, making him one of the best-selling conductors of all time. He was especially popular in the UK, where he had numerous hit records and was a frequent guest on television. *The Song from Moulin Rouge (Where Is Your Heart?)* is a popular song from the 1952 film *Moulin Rouge*. The song has a rich, romantic feel and features a sweeping melody played on strings, with a tender vocal performance. The song became a hit in the United States, reaching the top of the charts.

Oh Mein Papa

Eddie Calvert

Instrumental version by Eddie Calvert

Written by Paul Buckhard

This song was originally written in the 1940s for a stage musical, *Der Schwarze Hecht* (The Black Pike). In 1949 it became a European hit for Lys Assia, who later won the first ever Eurovision Song Contest with *Refrain* in 1956. In 1953 the British producer, Norrie Paramour, asked trumpeter Eddie Calvert to make an instrumental version. Despite being released as the B-side of the single *Mystery Street*, the song caught on and it became the first UK #1 to be recorded at EMI's Abbey Road studios. In the US, Eddie Fisher's vocal version topped the US charts and reached #9 in the UK, thus making it the first composition to chart as both instrumental and vocal in the UK. Eddie Calvert came to hate this song. According to *1000 UK #1 Hits* by Jon Kutner and Spencer Leigh, in the '70s Calvert said, "Hearing *Oh Mein Papa* is like having a 6-inch nail jammed through my head."

Top of the Pops in 1953

There were 15 number one records in 1953 in the UK single charts published by the NME. The best selling single of the year was *I Believe* by Frankie Laine.

		Weeks at number one
	**Here in my Heart** / Al Martino From 26th December 1952 for 3 weeks	
	**You Belong To Me** / Jo Stafford From 16th January 1953 for 1 week	
	**Comes A-Long A-Love** / Kay Starr From 23rd January 1953 for 1 week	
	**Outside of Heaven** / Eddie Fisher From 30th January 1953 for 1 week	
	**Don't Let the Stars Get in Your Eyes** / Perry Como From 6th February 1953 for 5 weeks	
	**She Wears Red Feathers** / Guy Mitchell From 13th March 1953 for 4 weeks	
	**Broken Wings** / The Stargazers From 10th April 1953 for 1 week	
	**How Much Is That Doggie in the Window?** / Lita Roza From 17th April 1953 for 1 week	
	**I Believe** / Frankie Laine From 24th Apr / 9 weeks then 3rd Jul / 6 weeks then 21st Aug / 3 weeks	
	**I'm Walking Behind You** / Eddie Fisher + Sally Sweetland From 26th June 1953 for 1 week	
	**The Song from Moulin Rouge** / Mantovani From 14th August 1953 for 1 week	
	**Look at That Girl** / Guy Mitchell From 11th September 1953 for 6 weeks	
	**Hey Joe** / Frankie Laine From 23rd October 1953 for 2 weeks	
	**Answer Me** / David Whitfield From 6th Nov / 1 week then joint No.1 on 11th Dec / 1 week	
	**Answer Me** / Frankie Laine From 13th November 1953 for 8 weeks until 8th January 1954	

The Original Benny Goodman Band and Trio (minus Benny Goodman!) and The Louis Armstrong All Stars

The original tour poster

When clarinettist Benny Goodman and trumpeter and vocalist, Louis Armstrong tried to map out how their 1953 joint US tour would play out, egos clashed and Goodman dropped out. Goodman's decision proved to be a stroke of luck for trumpeter Al Stewart. As the Goodman band without Goodman fell under the direction of a more laid back Gene Krupa, Al found himself developing a bond with Armstrong, a relationship that taught him about music, entertainment and life. Al spent seven weeks on the road with Armstrong and soon discovered that the trumpet great was a pragmatist with a gift for simplifying and enhancing the world around him. Al had always been confident about his own trumpet-playing abilities and style, but after touring with Armstrong and other greats on the tour, he had a new view of himself. By late May 1953 when the tour ended, Al had played shoulder to shoulder with legends and had held his own. Al Stewart later stated "I'm not a psychologist. Benny was the King of Swing. No one could touch him. But Louis was the Ambassador of Jazz to the world. Benny had all the talent to fill that very same role. But he had a different personality. He was a perfectionist and so demanding of himself. He put that feeling on everyone around him. He also was a bit aloof and emotionally sealed off. Louis was the complete opposite. It would have been such a wonderful thing had Benny and Louis gotten along in 1953 and Benny didn't drop out of the tour." Armstrong stole the show with numbers such as *St. Louis Blues*, *When the Saints Go Marching In* and *Weather Bird*. A big factor in the falling out between Goodman and Armstrong may have been Goodman's inability to adapt to new musical styles. Swing music quickly fell out of fashion as rock'n'roll and later pop came to the fore. Armstrong, on the other hand had a longer and more fruitful career, recording *Mack the Knife*, *Hello Dolly* and his poignant last hit single *What a Wonderful World*. The influence of Armstrong on the development of jazz is virtually immeasurable. His irrepressible personality both as a performer and as a public figure was so strong that to some it sometimes overshadowed his contributions as a musician and singer. In 1962, the Benny Goodman Orchestra (this time with Benny Goodman) toured the Soviet Union as part of a cultural exchange program between the two nations after the Cuban Missile Crisis and the end of that phase of the Cold War. Their visits was part of efforts to normalise relations between the United States and the USSR.

Benny Goodman

Louis Armstrong

Musical Highlights from the Coronation of Queen Elizabeth II

On Tuesday 2nd June 1953, the Coronation Ceremony at Westminster Abbey featured 40 pieces of music played before, during and after the ceremony itself. These included 9 new pieces of music written especially for the Coronation from the composers Arthur Bliss, William Walton, Herbert Howells, William Harris, George Dyson, Healey Willan, Vaughan Williams and Arnold Bax. Below are 8 selected pieces from the musical running order:

Zadok the Priest (Coronation Anthem No. 1) *by George Frideric Handel*
The text is derived from the biblical account of the anointing of Solomon by Zadok and the people's rejoicing at this event. These words have been used in every English coronation since that of King Edgar at Bath abbey in 973, and Handel's setting has been used at every British coronation since 1727.

Fantasia on Greensleeves *by Ralph Vaughan Williams*
The four-minute piece appeared originally in Vaughan Williams's 1928 opera *Sir John in Love*. The piece also incorporates a folk song called *Lovely Joan* which Vaughan Williams came across in Sussex.

I Was Glad *by Hubert Parry*
From the first few brassy opening notes on the organ to the triumphant full choir, Parry managed to fill the piece with choral ecstasy and prayerful reverence in equal measure in a piece lasting just over 5 minutes.

Coronation March: 'Orb and Sceptre' *by William Walton*
A fantastically royal piece from William Walton, which received its premiere at the Coronation. It calls to mind the 'Globus cruciger' (or, cross-bearing orb) held by monarchs through the ages, symbolising Christ's authority over the world.

Nimrod (from Enigma Variations) *by Edward Elgar*
Elgar's main theme is harmonised using tension-building dissonant chords. However, the dissonance is resolved in one of the chords that follows.

Coronation Te Deum for chorus, orchestra and organ *by William Walton*
A piece that utilised all the Queen's trumpeters and a full boys' choir. It is one of Walton's most elegant works.

Pomp and Circumstance March No. 1 in D *by Edward Elgar*
The title comes from Shakespeare's *Othello* (the "pride, pomp and circumstance of glorious war" from Act III, Scene 3)

Belshazzar's Feast *by William Walton*
First performed at the Leeds Festival in 1931.

Review of the Year

1953 was an important year for English language literature, marked by the publication of several notable works across a variety of genres. One of the most significant literary events of the year was the release of Ian Fleming's first James Bond novel, *Casino Royale*, which would go on to become a global phenomenon and spawn a multi-billion-dollar film franchise. Other notable works published included John Wyndham's post-apocalyptic novel *The Kraken Wakes* and Ray Bradbury's dystopian work *Fahrenheit 451*. In children's literature, C.S. Lewis produced the fourth book in the Narnia series, *The Silver Chair*. Enid Blyton wrote the twelfth book in the Famous Five series, *Five Go down to the Sea*. This time the adventurous quintet find themselves in Cornwall where they learn about wreckers. In the world of poetry, Dylan Thomas's death led to a surge in sales of his *Collected Poems*, published in 1952, which cemented his reputation as one of the most important poets of his generation. His untimely death also left his novel, *Adventures in the Skin Trade*, unfinished. Meanwhile, Samuel Beckett's play *Waiting for Godot* premiered in Paris, marking a turning point in modernist drama with its exploration of the absurdity of existence. On the other side of the Atlantic, Arthur Miller produced his critique on McCarthyism, *The Crucible*. In the world of the visual arts, Robert Rauschenberg created his famous *Erased de Kooning Drawing*, which consisted of a drawing by Willem de Kooning that Rauschenberg had erased, leaving only faint traces of the original image. This piece was a statement on the nature of artistic creation and the idea that art can be created through the act of destruction. Meanwhile de Kooning was more constructive in his art, producing *Woman III*, part of a series of six abstract expressionist paintings. Also in America, Edward Hopper's *Office in a Small City* went on display. The painting depicts a man sitting in a corner office surveying the landscape outdoors, once more exploring Hopper's recurring theme of loneliness in an urban environment. In sculpture, two of the greatest artists of the twentieth century were at the height of their creative powers. Henry Moore produced his iconic *Draped Reclining Woman*. The artist's copy is on display in the garden of his old house in Perry Green, Hertfordshire. Barbara Hepworth produced one of her series of sculptures entitled *Hieroglyph* – a play on the word's true meaning, heiros meaning sacred and glyphein, meaning to carve. She summed up her philosophy when she stated that she was "sick of sculptures in galleries and photos with flat backgrounds .... no sculpture really lives until it goes back to the landscape, the trees, air and clouds."

Author Ray Bradbury

American Playwright Arthur Miller

Sculptor Henry Moore (pictured in 1973)

Casino Royale

Author: Ian Fleming   First published in 1953

This was the first book in the James Bond series. The story follows the adventures of Bond, a British secret agent, as he travels to the Casino Royale in France to take part in a high-stakes card game with Le Chiffre, a notorious financier of international terrorism. Bond is aided by Vesper Lynd, a beautiful government agent, but their partnership is complicated by the threat of Le Chiffre and his accomplices. The book is full of action, espionage and romance, and it establishes the characteristics and themes that would define the Bond franchise for decades to come. The writing is brisk and atmospheric, capturing the glamour and danger of the Cold War era. It also explores Bond's emotional and psychological journey, as he begins to question his loyalty to his government and his place in the world. The novel is set against a backdrop of political tensions and international espionage, with the threat of the Cold War hanging over every scene.

Fahrenheit 451

Author: Ray Bradbury   Published: 19th October 1953

The burning of books is such an effective tool for controlling the population, so the message of Ray Bradbury's book is scarily real. If society's wisdom could be taken away, then so could their freedom. If knowledge was burnt, then the people would be left in a complete state of innocent ignorance. Books have become illegal; thus, owning them is a form of disobedience against the state and a violation of the law. The books are burnt by a special group of firefighters, yes firefighters, which hunts readers mercilessly and burns their houses along with their books. One woman burns with her books by her own choosing rather than submit to ignorance. The firefighters don't know exactly why they do it, they just do it unflinchingly because that is what they are told to do. Guy Montag is one such firefighter. He's miserable living a mundane life with his partner. He burns books without thinking until one day an innocent young girl changes his life forever.

Go Tell It On The Mountain

Author: James Baldwin   First published in 1953

The book tells the story of John Grimes, a young Black man growing up in Harlem, New York in the 1930s. John is the stepson of a Pentecostal minister, and the novel revolves around his struggles with faith, identity and family. Baldwin uses a non-linear narrative to explore John's past and present, delving into the histories of his parents and grandparents to create a complex and layered portrait of the Grimes family. Through John's journey, the novel explores themes of racism, religion, sexuality, and cross-generational trauma. Baldwin's vivid and evocative prose captures the rhythms and tensions of Black life in Harlem during a time of immense social and cultural change. The novel is a powerful and deeply personal exploration of the struggles and joys of Black identity, and a testament to Baldwin's skill as a writer and his commitment to telling the stories of those who have been marginalised and oppressed by mainstream society.

The Kraken Wakes

Author: John Wyndham First published in 1953

The novel tells the story of an alien invasion of Earth, which takes the form of a series of undersea eruptions that cause catastrophic damage to coastal cities and shipping. It is structured as a first-person narrative by the protagonist, journalist Mike Watson, and his wife, Phyllis. As the world is plunged into chaos and governments struggle to understand the nature of the threat, Mike and Phyllis become involved in the efforts to repel the invaders and save humanity. Wyndham's writing is characterised by a focus on the psychological impact of extraordinary events on ordinary people, and *The Kraken Wakes* is no exception. As the world descends into panic and conflict, the novel explores themes of communication, cooperation and the relationship between humanity and the natural world. The book paints vivid descriptions of the alien threat and the gradual escalation of tension, as well as its prescient commentary on the potential dangers of environmental degradation and the impact of human activity on the planet.

The Night of the Hunter

Author: Davis Grubb First published in 1953

The story is set in West Virginia during the Great Depression and follows two children who become the target of a dangerous and deranged preacher named Harry Powell. Powell, who believes he is doing the work of God, has recently been released from prison and is on the hunt for $10,000 that his former cellmate had stolen and hidden before being arrested. He tracks down the man's widow, Willa, and convinces her to marry him in order to get access to the money. However, Willa's children, John and Pearl, become wary of Powell and his motives. As Powell's true intentions become clear, John and Pearl are forced to flee for their lives, navigating the harsh terrain and dangerous characters of the Depression-era South. The plot was based on the true story of Harry Powers, who was hanged in 1932 for the murders of two widows and three children. In 1955 it was adapted for cinema with Robert Mitchum starring as Harry Powell.

A Pocket Full of Rye

Author: Agatha Christie First published in 1953

Rex Fortescue is a ruthless business man with questionable practices. When he suddenly falls ill and dies after drinking his regular cup of tea at his office, the police suspect foul play. Inspector Neele visits Yewtree Lodge, Mr. Fortescue's home, to interview the family and staff. Between a younger second wife, a son with whom Mr. Fortescue was currently at odds, a daughter who wished to marry but the fiancée was not approved by dad and a whole slew of characters with the staff, Inspector Neele has no shortage of suspects and an abundance of motives. Miss Marple reads about the murder in the papers and after another twist in the case, gets involved. As per usual with Christie, there are plenty of red herrings and misdirections. As the investigation progresses, Miss Marple inserts herself into the case and soon links the murder to a rhyme. Uncovering a complex plot, Miss Marple unmasks the culprit.

The Silver Chair

Author: C.S. Lewis Published: 7th September 1953

This was the fourth book in the *Chronicles of Narnia*. The story follows two children, Eustace Scrubb and Jill Pole, as they are transported to the magical land of Narnia. They are tasked by Aslan to find Prince Rilian, the son of King Caspian, who has been missing for many years. The pair embark on a dangerous journey across the land, encountering many obstacles and enemies along the way. They are joined by a talking Marsh-wiggle named Puddleglum, who helps them navigate through the treacherous Underland and ultimately find Prince Rilian. The book explores themes of courage, loyalty and the importance of believing in things that cannot be seen. It is a beloved classic of children's literature and continues to captivate readers of all ages with its imaginative storytelling and timeless messages. *The Silver Chair* was adapted and filmed as a BBC television series of six episodes in 1990.

Childhood's End

Author: Arthur C. Clarke First published in 1953

"Men called them Overlords. They had come from outer space— they had brought peace and prosperity to Earth. But then the change began."

The novel is set in the near future and explores the idea of the evolution of the human species and the eventual end of childhood. In the story, an advanced alien race known as the Overlords arrives on Earth and takes control, bringing about a period of peace and prosperity. They also oversee the next stage in human evolution, which results in a new form of humanity. The novel explores themes such as the nature of human evolution, the relationship between humanity and extraterrestrial life and the role of technology in human development. It has been praised for its thought-provoking ideas and imaginative world-building, as well as its commentary on the nature of power and the dangers of technological advancement. It is as relevant today, if not more so, than when it was written.

The Go-Between

Author: L.P. Hartley First published in 1953

"The past is a foreign country; they do things differently there." The story is told by Leo, a middle-aged man looking back on the fateful summer of 1900, when he was twelve years old. He accepts an invitation to spend a few weeks with the family of Marcus Maudsley, one of his school chums. The Maudsleys live in Brandham Hall, a grand country house in Norfolk. The middle class Leo is totally unaccustomed to their affluent lifestyle. He quickly develops a crush on Marian, the beautiful older sister of Marcus. Eager to please, he becomes her "postman", taking secret messages to Ted Burgess, a local farmer. Leo is initially unaware of the relationship between Ted and Marian, but the truth gradually dawns on him, and his efforts to extricate himself from this tricky situation have profound consequences for all involved. The story also examines class in an interesting way - a cricket match between Brandham Hall and the local villagers provides an intriguing glimpse into the distinctions and habits of the two groups.

The characters Vladimir and Estragon in Waiting for Godot

Waiting for Godot

Written by Samuel Beckett
Premiered 5th January 1953 at the Théâtre de Babylone, Paris
(The English-language version premiered in London in 1955)

The play revolves around two tramps, Vladimir and Estragon, who spend their time waiting for the arrival of a mysterious figure named Godot. Despite the fact that they are not sure what Godot represents or why they are waiting for him, the two characters pass the time by engaging in conversation and contemplating the meaning of life. The play is widely considered to be one of the most influential works of 20th century theatre, and is often referred to as a masterpiece of the Theatre of the Absurd. This genre of theatre is characterised by its focus on the absurdity of existence and the human condition, often exploring themes of waiting, boredom and the search for meaning. One of the key features of *Waiting for Godot* is its open-ended nature, with the play leaving many questions unanswered. This has led to a wide range of interpretations and analyses of the play, with scholars and critics offering a range of explanations of the play's meaning and purpose. When Peter Hall directed the English language version at the Arts Theatre in London in 1955, he said "I haven't really the foggiest idea what some of it means... But if we stop and discuss every line we'll never open." In a poll conducted by the British Royal National Theatre in 1998/99, it was voted the most significant English-language play of the 20th century.

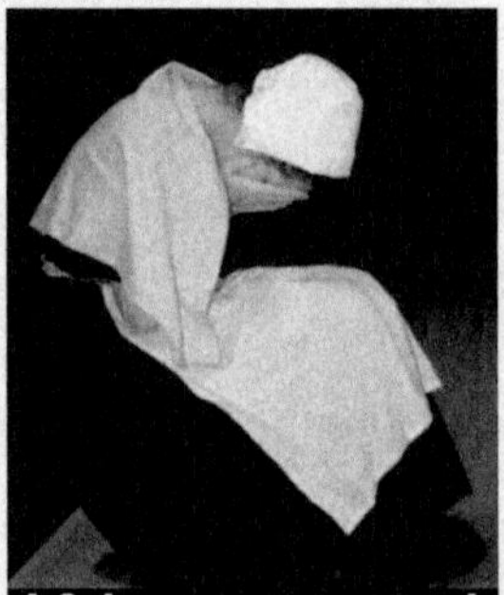

A Salem woman accused of witchcraft in The Crucible

The Crucible

Written by Arthur Miller
Premiered 22nd January 1953
At The Martin Beck Theatre, New York

The play is set in the Puritan community of Salem, Massachusetts during the late 17th century and is based on the real-life events of the Salem Witch Trials. The play explores the themes of hysteria, mob mentality and the consequences of power and manipulation. The central conflict revolves around the accusatory claims of witchcraft made by a group of young girls against members of the Salem community. As the accusations and trials escalate, the play delves into the motivations of the accusers and the characters caught in their web of deceit. *The Crucible* is widely regarded as a masterpiece of American theatre, and has been praised for its insightful commentary on the dangers of mass hysteria and the human capacity for cruelty and manipulation. The play has been interpreted as an allegory for the Red Scare and the McCarthy Era, in which Miller himself was implicated for his political beliefs. In addition to its political and social commentary, *The Crucible* is also praised for its powerful performances and compelling characters. Through the characters of John Proctor, Abigail Williams and Elizabeth Proctor, Miller explores the complexities of human nature, including the struggle between truth and personal morality. Today, it remains a widely performed and highly regarded work of theatre. The many stage and screen adaptations of the play include a film in 1996 starring Winona Ryder and Daniel Day-Lewis.

The Royal Variety Performance 1953

In front of Her Majesty the Queen and the Duke of Edinburgh
On 2nd November 1953
at the London Coliseum Theatre

Her Majesty the Queen, the Duke of Edinburgh and Princess Margaret attended the Coronation Year Royal Variety Performance at the Coliseum, with the Duke wearing horn-rimmed glasses for the first time in public. Invited to offer a professional opinion on the reason for this, a leading London oculist suggested, "It seems likely that the Duke may be suffering from a very common complaint - slightly short sight." The immensely successful production of *Guys and Dolls* was playing at the Coliseum at the time. Several numbers were included in the programme resulting in some delicate changes to aspects of the production which it was felt might possibly cause offence in some religious quarters. As Harry Marlow, secretary of the Variety Artistes' Benevolent Fund, explained, "These performances attract people of all religions and we do not want anything to offend." Thus, the Salvation Army uniforms in the show were changed on the night to skirts and blouses, the words "Save-a-Soul Mission" were discreetly dropped and several other minor amendments were made. The composer Frank Loesser, was slightly puzzled by the somewhat bizarre permutations. "There seem to have been some strange cuts," he commented. "While the word 'heaven' has been changed to 'judgement', apparently the phrase 'heavenly trip' is permissible." Over the years several commentators have observed that performances at Royal Variety Shows have perhaps lacked the uninhibited display seen by other audiences. If this is true, it merely reflects the very great care taken by the producers to ensure that nothing is admitted that could possibly be misconstrued. Perhaps Bud Flanagan expressed this understanding of the special status of the Royal Variety Performance most succinctly when he said after one show, "Protocol must be observed, and everyone on and off the stage must respect it. Whatever some stars may think of themselves, at a Royal Show the top of the bill is the Monarch and we the artistes have the privilege of performing in support." One of the most accomplished acts of the evening was that of Max Bygraves. The Stage said of him: "among the newcomers to variety, outstanding is Max Bygraves, who was unknown less than ten years ago. He has his own sense of comedy, which he is able to communicate in an individual way." For comedian Jimmy Edwards this was his third Royal Variety Performance in three years. He took the opportunity afterwards to reflect on the problems of appearing in such shows. "It is a great worry and something of a risk", he said, "and sometimes I wonder what it is all about. You cannot help wondering if you can possibly succeed with this very difficult and unrepresentative audience."

STARS MEET QUEEN ELIZABETH

Two members of the cast of "Guys and Dolls," Vivian Blaine and Sam Levene, are shown as they were presented to Queen Elizabeth after a royal variety performance of the show at the London Coliseum. In background, the Duke of Edinburgh greets Jimmy James and Eve Boswell.

A newspaper clipping following The Royal Variety Performance

Jimmy Edwards

Barbara Hepworth & Henry Moore

Barbara Hepworth and Henry Moore were two of the most influential British artists of the 20th century. They were both sculptors who contributed significantly to the development of modern art and the abstract movement. While they shared many similarities in their artistic styles and careers, they also had some notable differences. Barbara Hepworth was born in Wakefield, Yorkshire in 1903, and Henry Moore was born in Castleford, Yorkshire in 1898. Both artists were influenced by the natural landscape of their home region, which can be seen in their works. Hepworth studied at Leeds School of Art and then at the Royal College of Art in London. Moore also studied at the Royal College of Art but his studies were temporarily interrupted by military service during World War I. Both artists were also inspired by the works of Constantin Brancusi and Pablo Picasso, as well as the ancient cultures of Africa and Mexico. Hepworth's early works were figurative, but she gradually moved towards abstraction and began to incorporate elements of the landscape into her sculptures. She became associated with the British abstract movement, which emphasised simplicity, geometry and the use of pure forms. She was one of the few female artists who achieved significant success in this male-dominated field. Her works were often made of materials such as marble, bronze and wood and featured smooth, organic shapes. Moore's early works were also figurative, but he too gradually moved towards abstraction. He is perhaps best known for his large, abstract sculptures of reclining figures. His works were often made of materials such as bronze, stone and wood and featured rough, organic shapes. Moore was also interested in the relationship between the sculpture and its environment, and many of his works were designed to be displayed outdoors. Despite their similarities, Hepworth and Moore had different approaches to sculpture. Hepworth's works were often more intimate and delicate, while Moore's were more monumental and forceful. Hepworth was more interested in the inner qualities of the materials she used, while Moore focused more on the outer shapes they created. Both artists, however, were deeply committed to the idea that sculpture could convey emotions and ideas in a way that was different from other forms of art. In 1953, Hepworth produced one of her series of sculptures entitled *Hieroglyph* and Moore produced one of his finest works *Draped Reclining Woman*.

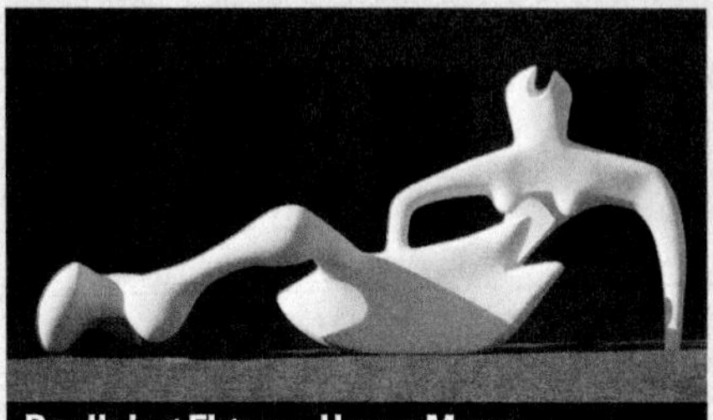

Reclining Figure - Henry Moore

Single Form - Barbara Hepworth

Draped Reclining Woman - Henry Moore

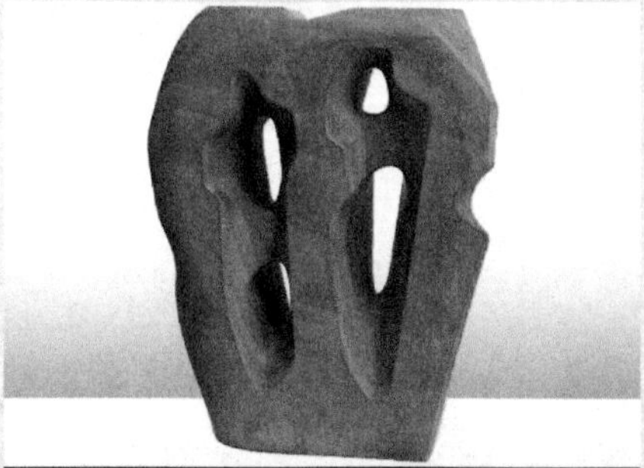

Hieroglyph - Barbara Hepworth

John Masefield, Poet Laureate (served 1930-1967)

John Masefield

Masefield was the longest serving Poet Laureate to serve entirely within the 20th century. His 37 years of service was only beaten by Alfred, Lord Tennyson who held the post between 1850-1892. By the 1950s Masefield seemed to be from a bygone era as traditional poetry had fallen out of favour as more modernist poets such as Sylvia Plath and Stevie Smith were gaining more traction. The emerging Beat Generation of poets such as Ginsburg, Carr and Huncke seemed to speak more to the youth of the day than did the rather staid Masefield. Still, he took his job seriously and acted as all good Poets Laureate do. He wrote poems for the court, in his case the House of Windsor. Rather quaintly Masefield would send his poems to the Times of London for their approval with a stamped addressed envelope for their response. Even though he seemed more like a 19th century poet than most of his contemporaries, many of his poems still stand the test of time. His *Sonnets and Poems* written in the midst of World War I and *A Generation Risen* written during World War II defined him as a chronicler of British 20th century history and one of the few poets to have written during both wars. Author Muriel Spark published a biography of John Masefield in 1953.

The Role of Poet Laureate Through The Ages

The monarch of the day bestows the honorary position of Poet Laureate, currently on the advice of the prime minister. There are no specific duties to the role although it is expected that the holder produces original verse to commemorate significant national occasions. The first official Poet Laureate was John Dryden who was appointed by Charles II in 1668. Until Andrew Motion was appointed in 1999 the laureateship was held for life; subsequently the position has been offered for a fixed term of 10 years. Other notable Poet Laureates included William Wordsworth (1843-1850), Sir John Betjeman (1972-1984) and Ted Hughes (1984-1998). The actor Daniel Day-Lewis's father, Cecil, was also Poet Laureate from 1968 to 1972.It was only in 2009 that the first woman, Carol Ann Duffy, was offered the role. She was also the first Scot.

Sir John Betjeman

Carol Ann Duffy

The role of Poet Laureate is not a money spinner; Andrew Motion and Carol Ann Duffy were offered annual salaries of £5,750 per year. However, in a quirky tradition dating back to Charles I, the holder also receives a barrel of sherry.

The Battle for Mach 2

Chuck Yeager's Bell XS-1

During World War 2 both the United Kingdom and the United States initiated top secret projects to develop an aircraft capable of breaking the sound barrier. The US project was contracted to the Bell Aircraft company by the US Army Air Forces (USAAF) and the National Advisory Committee for Aeronautics (NACA). They developed an aircraft codenamed XS-1 (Experimental, Supersonic) which was essentially a bullet with wings. Its aerodynamic design was similar to a Browning .50 calibre machine bullet; propulsion was provided by a rocket motor. With the UK project delayed the US project would see testing commence in January 1946. Then on the 14th October 1947 over the Mojave Desert in California, Captain Charles 'Chuck' Yeager was released from the bomb bays doors of a B-29 bomber on-board his Bell XS-1. He fired up the rocket motor and reached a top speed of 700mph (Mach 1.06) and went into the records book as the first person to break the sound barrier in an airplane. Whilst the USAAF was interested in developing supersonic aircraft for combat operations, NACA's interest was in the understanding of supersonic and high altitude flight. In the late 1940's and early 1950's their programs diverged and ended up competing with each other as to who would hold the air speed record. In 1953 the goal was to become the first to fly at Mach 2, twice the speed of sound. NACA were victorious when, on 20th November 1953, nearly 50 years after the first ever powered flight, pilot Scott Crossfield flew his Douglas Skyrocket at Mach 2.005. However, Chuck Yeager and the USAAF were determined to beat it before the year was out. In a project known as "Operation NACA Weep", Yeager climbed on-board his second generation Bell X-1A aircraft just 22 days later on 12th December 1953 flying it up to a colossal altitude of nearly 80,000 feet. Here in level flight he pushed his aircraft to a staggering speed of 1620mph, Mach 2.44 thereby smashing the record. However, the flight almost ended in catastrophe as Yeager lost control of the X-1A and it span out of control losing 51,000 feet in less than a minute due to a little known phenomena called inertia coupling. Such were the piloting skills of Yeager, he was able to regain control of the aircraft and land safely. This flight both earned him a Distinguished Service Medal and the title of "fastest man alive". Yeager continued to have a long and highly distinguished career with his legacy as a pioneering aviator continuing to inspire future generations of pilots and astronauts. He passed away in 2020 at the age of 97.

Captain Charles 'Chuck' Yeager

The Bell X-1A

The Rockoon

Just after World War II ended German V-2 rocket technology was re-purposed by the United States to conduct scientific research at the outer reaches of earth's atmosphere and beyond. Due to the expense of assembling V-2 rockets and the limited supply of parts, a new dedicated rocket design was sought. This led to a project headed by James Van Allen at the Applied Physics Laboratory. His team created the Aerobee, a so-called sounding rocket, capable of delivering scientific instruments into sub-orbital space. It was during an Aerobee launch in 1949 that James Van Allen and his team discussed the idea of using helium balloons to lift the rocket up to high altitude before firing to enable even higher altitudes to be reached. The idea for the 'Rockoon' (Rocket + Balloon) was born. After initial problems with rocket engines failing to fire at altitude, the first successful launch was on 9th August 1953 out in the Atlantic Ocean. Launches are required far away from populated areas for safety reasons as the rockoons are unguided. The initial programme gathered huge amounts of data leading to a greater understanding of the earth's outer atmosphere. In the last few years rockoons are once again in fashion as many companies are viewing them as a low cost route to deploying satellites into low Earth orbit.

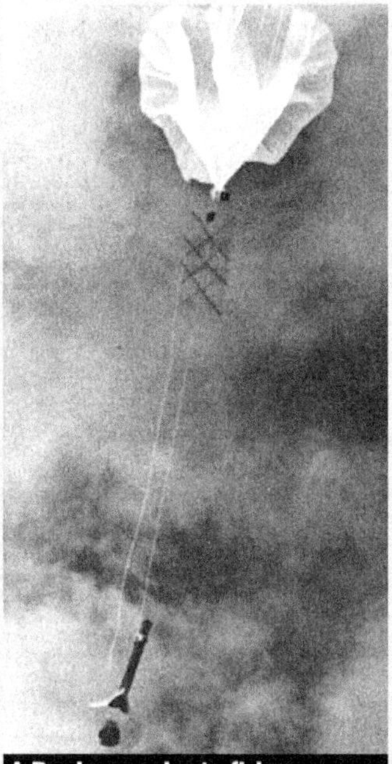
A Rockoon prior to firing

The PGM-11 Redstone Ballistic Missile

Redstone missile launch preparations

Another descendant of the German V-2 rocket programme was the development of the Redstone rocket family. In 1945, the United States created a top secret intelligence program codenamed Operation Paperclip which saw over 1,600 German scientists, engineers and technicians brought to the US to work for government departments. Led by German rocket engineer Wernher von Braun, a program was set up by the Army Ballistic Missile Agency (ABMA) to develop a short-range tactical ballistic missile capable of carrying live nuclear warheads. On the 20th August 1953 the first Redstone test took place at Cape Canaveral, Florida. The missile flew for 80 seconds before engine failure struck and it fell into the sea. Further tests were more successful with the PGM-11 Redstones entering active service in 1958 where they were deployed in West Germany as part of Nato's Cold War defence of Western Europe. The same year saw the first detonation with a live nuclear warhead in a high altitude test known as Operation Hardtack I. The Redstone missile was further developed and used as a launch vehicle in 1961 propelling astronaut Alan Shepherd to become the first American in space.

The Structure of DNA

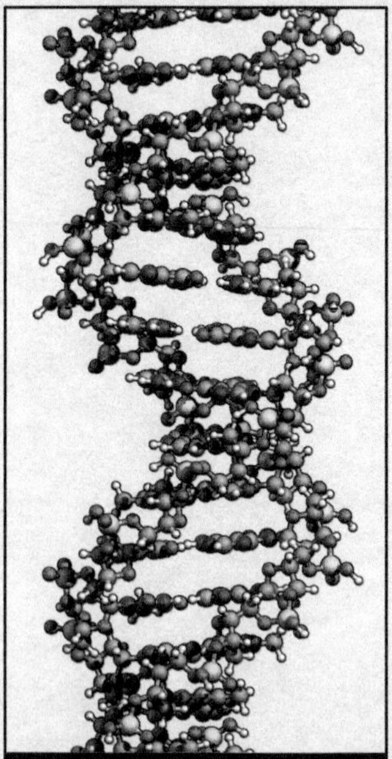
DNA's double helix structure

In 1953 at the Cavendish Laboratory at Cambridge University, James Watson and Francis Crick made a groundbreaking discovery that changed the field of biology forever. They determined the structure of DNA, which is the molecule responsible for carrying genetic information in all living organisms. Their discovery was published in the journal *Nature* on 25th April 1953, in a short article titled "Molecular Structure of Nucleic Acids: A Structure for Deoxyribose Nucleic Acid." Watson and Crick used a combination of X-ray crystallography data and model building to propose the structure of DNA. They found that it was made up of two strands of nucleotides that twisted around each other to form a double helix. Their discovery was a major breakthrough in understanding how genetic information is stored and passed down from one generation to the next. It also provided a basis for understanding how mutations in DNA can lead to genetic diseases and has had far-reaching implications, from advances in genetics to the development of new technologies such as DNA sequencing. Watson and Crick's work remains one of the most significant scientific achievements of the 20th century. However, the story was not without controversy and tragedy. To find out more, see page 75 in the next chapter.

The First Human Trials of the Salk Polio Vaccine

Newspapers reporting the success of the Joseph Salk polio vaccine. By the early 1960's Salk's injected vaccine was replaced by an oral vaccine.

Polio, also known as poliomyelitis, is a highly infectious viral disease that primarily affects children under the age of five. The virus attacks the nervous system, leading to paralysis, muscle weakness, and even death in some cases. In the 20th century, polio was a major health concern, and outbreaks were common in many countries. In the 1930's British-born virologist Maurice Brodie developed one of the first vaccines based on an inactive form of the polio virus, which stimulated the immune system to produce antibodies without causing the disease. Early human trials were inconclusive plus Brodie tragically died suddenly of a heart attack aged only 36. In the early 1950's the American virologist Joseph Salk developed an inactivated vaccine based on Brodie's work. After successful laboratory tests on animals in 1952 he conducted the first human trials in 1953 including on himself, his wife and his three children. He announced the success of these initial human trials on national radio on 26th March 1953. This led, in 1954, to the largest medical experiment in history where over a million children were administered the vaccine. In 1955 the Salk polio vaccine was granted a public licence.

The First Open Heart Surgery using Cardiopulmonary Bypass

John Heysham Gibbon

John Heysham Gibbon was born on 29th September 1903 in Philadelphia, Pennsylvania. He grew up in a medical family; his father was a renowned surgeon and his mother was a nurse. Gibbon earned his medical degree from Jefferson Medical College in 1927 and went on to pursue research in the field of cardiothoracic surgery. He began working on the development of the heart-lung machine in the 1930s, following the death of a close friend who had died of a pulmonary embolism during surgery. Gibbon's work on the heart-lung machine was largely motivated by a desire to find a safer way to perform surgery on the heart and lungs. He spent over 20 years perfecting the device before performing the first successful open-heart surgery using cardiopulmonary bypass in 1953. The patient was an 18-year-old girl with a congenital heart defect called atrial septal defect, which is a hole in the wall separating the two upper chambers of the heart. The surgery involved stopping the heart and connecting the patient to the heart-lung machine, which oxygenated and circulated her blood while the defect was repaired. The procedure was a success and the patient recovered fully. She would go on to live for more than 30 years. Gibbon's invention revolutionised the field of cardiac surgery and made it possible to perform more complex procedures on the heart and lungs including bypasss surgery and heart transplantation.

The Discovery of REM Sleep

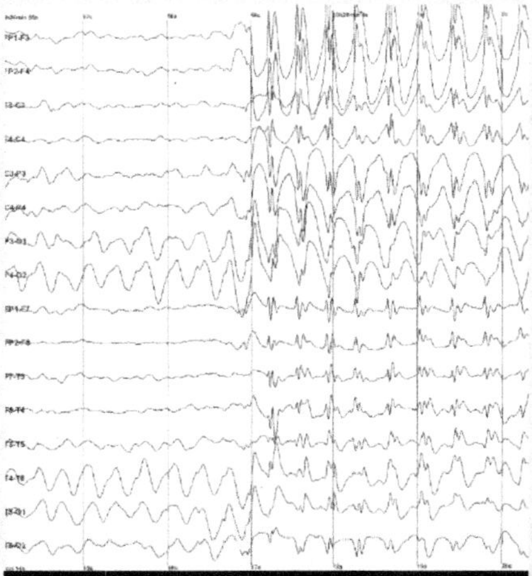

An electroencephalogram trace

Nathaniel Kleitman was the Professor Emeritus in Physiology at the University of Chicago. He is recognised at the father of modern sleep research. In 1953, one of Kleitman's students, Eugene Aserinsky, conducted sleep experiments on volunteers who were connected to an electroencephalogram machine. During the night the machine would record the electrical activity of the brain on a roll of paper measuring half a mile in length. Aserinsky observed that multiple times per night the sleeper's eyes would move frantically back and forth. Kleitman asked that the experiment be repeated but this time on his own daughter, Esther. Kleitman and Aserinsky deduced that these periods of rapid eye movement correlated to increased brain activity whilst the sleeper was in a vivid dreaming state. During REM sleep, the brain is highly active and consumes more oxygen than during wakefulness, despite the body being in a state of paralysis. This has led it to be know as "paradoxical sleep". REM sleep is more prevalent in infants and young children, with babies spending up to 50% of their sleep time in REM. As we age, the amount of time spent in REM decreases. A tragic and ironic footnote to their discovery is that in 1998 Eugene Aserinsky, aged 77, died in a car accident when his car hit a tree. The autopsy was inconclusive leading to the possibility that he had fallen asleep at the wheel.

The Dawn of Colour Television

The Westinghouse H840CK15

In the USA, two rival companies were racing to become the first mass producer of colour TV's. They were Westinghouse and RCA. In December 1953 RCA manufactured a series of 200 colour receivers which were provided to NBC affiliates and RCA distributors in readiness for "The First Rose Parade Color Cast" on 1st January 1954. Broadcast from east coast to west coast, this was the first ever full colour television broadcast. It featured the New Year's Day 'Tournament of the Roses' parade in Pasadena, California. Despite this success it was Westinghouse who managed to get their colour televisions sets on sale to the public first in March 1954. They cost $1295 which was approximately half the price of a family car. A few weeks later RCA put their model CT-100 on sale at a price point of $1000. Sales were sluggish due to the prohibitively high price and small screen size. However the RCA model did sell in the thousands meaning that RCA could claim the prize of selling the first mass produced colour television. It took another 13 years before colour TV's first went on sale in the UK. Until this point, British manufacturers had dominated the UK television market, but 1969 saw the arrival of Sony with its Trinitron colour television. It became a market leader and marked the arrival of Japan as a world leader in electronics leaving British manufacturers struggling to compete.

The First Domestic Washer-Dryer

Advertising for the 1953 Bendix Duomatic

The Bendix Duomatic, introduced in the USA in 1953, was the first washer-dryer combination unit designed for home use. This innovation brought convenience to households by allowing clothes to be washed and dried in a single machine, saving time and space. It featured a front-loading drum that allowed for larger loads than top-loading washers. Additionally, the machine was equipped with a heater that dried clothes using hot air. This was a significant advancement from traditional washing machines that required clothes to be hung outside to dry. Another important innovation was the incorporation of a condenser system that collected and evaporated moisture from the dryer cycle, eliminating the need for external venting, further expanding its marketability. Today, most households have a washing machine and a separate dryer, but the Bendix Duomatic paved the way for the integration of laundry appliances. Its innovations have also influenced the design of modern washing machines and dryers, making laundry an easier and more efficient household chore.

Cinemascope

Cinemascope logo from the credits of 'The High And The Mighty'

In the early 1950's cinema attendance was in decline due to the rise of television. Film production companies used technical innovation to fight back. In 1952, Cinerama and 3D were first launched. Faced with this new competition, head of 20th Century Fox, Spyros Skouras, asked his technical department to develop a format that would wow cinema audiences. It also needed to be cost effectively retrofitted into existing cinemas, unlike the Cinerama format. The Fox engineers looked back in history to the 1920s and to the work of French engineer and inventor, Henri Chrétien, who developed the Anamorphoscope in 1926. His system used an optical trick that produced images that were twice as wide as those produced by conventional lenses. The optical company, Bausch and Lomb created a special 'anamorphoser' lens for Fox based on Chrétien's design, that allowed widescreen images of 2.55:1 to be projected. The first film produced in this new cinemascope format was *The Robe* (see the Entertainment Chapter). The new format proved a hit with audiences. Walt Disney would go on to licence the format using it in films such as *Lady and the Tramp* and *20,000 Leagues under the Sea.* The influential motion picture company, Panavision, was also founded in 1953 due to the demand for Cinemascope cameras and lense equipment.

3D Footage of the Queen's Coronation

The Coronation Procession in 1953

For over 50 years one of the biggest secrets of the coronation of Queen Elizabeth II lay hidden in the dusty vaults of the British Film Institute. In 1953, Bob Angell and Arthur Wooster were two innovative, young British cameramen who operated rare and highly specialised 3D colour camera equipment. They were commissioned by Pathé Newsreel to capture moments from the Coronation using their equipment with the hope that it would be shown in 3D in cinemas. On the day, Bob and Arthur captured footage of the procession to and from Westminster Abbey. They also captured footage from the Queen and the Duke of Edinburgh's visit to the Derby and their trip on the Royal Barge down the River Thames. However, it subsequently proved too complex and costly to show the film in British cinemas, so it was never shown in public. It was only when Arthur Wooster casually mentioned the existence of this film to his son, David, some 56 years later that was it discovered in the BFI vaults. The footage was restored and shown on television for the first time in 2009. The Queen was so thrilled to hear of this discovery, she invited the friends, now in their 80's, to capture new footage of a Royal garden party to add to the original.

The Conquest of Everest

Mount Everest

Sir Edmund Hillary of New Zealand and Tenzing Norgay of Nepal were the first climbers to successfully reach the summit of Mount Everest, the highest peak in the world, on the 29th May 1953. The expedition was led by John Hunt of the British Mount Everest Expedition team. Hillary and Tenzing began their final ascent from the South Col, a flat section of the mountain located at an altitude of around 26,000 feet. The two climbers, along with their Sherpa guide Ang Nyima, had spent the night at the South Col before setting out for the summit early in the morning. They faced many obstacles and challenges on their way up the mountain, including treacherous ice and snow, strong winds and thin air. They also had to navigate what became known as the "Hillary Step", a steep, rocky section of the mountain that proved difficult to climb. Despite these challenges, Hillary and Tenzing pressed on and reached the summit at 11:30 am. They spent only 15 minutes there, taking photographs and absorbing the breathtaking view before beginning their descent. Their successful ascent was a major achievement, not only for the climbers themselves, but also for the entire climbing community. It was the first time anyone had reached the summit of Mount Everest and the achievement was celebrated around the world. The expedition was also a milestone for Nepal, which had been closed off to foreigners for many years. The successful climb helped to open up the country to the outside world and boost tourism. The achievement of Hillary and Tenzing also helped to bring attention to the Sherpa people, the ethnic group from the region that provided vital support for the expedition. Tenzing, a Sherpa himself, became a hero in his native Nepal and around the world. In the years following their climb, both men continued to be active in the mountaineering community. Hillary went on to lead several other expeditions, including an attempt to climb the unclimbed mountain of Cho Oyu in Tibet. He also became involved in various humanitarian and conservation efforts in Nepal. Tenzing, meanwhile, continued to work as a guide and also became a spokesman for the Nepalese government. The achievement of Hillary and Tenzing sparked a renewed interest in climbing Mount Everest, with many other climbers attempting to reach the summit in the years that followed. However, the climb remains a dangerous and challenging endeavour, and many climbers have lost their lives attempting to reach the summit. Throughout the years since the first ascent more than 300 people have died on Everest. Despite the risks, climbing Mount Everest remains a popular pursuit, with hundreds of climbers attempting to reach the summit each year. The climb is also a major source of revenue for Nepal, with climbers paying thousands of dollars for the opportunity to attempt the ascent. News of the conquest of the world's highest mountain was released by the Times newspaper on the morning of the 2nd June 1953, the day of Queen Elizabeth II's Coronation.

Edmund Hillary and Tenzing Norgay after their Mount Everest ascent on the 29th May 1953

Decoding The Structure of DNA

James Watson (left) and Francis Crick (right)

In 1953, James Watson and Francis Crick published a paper in the journal *Nature* describing their decoding of the double helix structure of DNA. Their discovery was based on the work of Rosalind Franklin and Maurice Wilkins, who had used X-ray crystallography to produce high-resolution images of DNA fibres. Watson and Crick were able to use Franklin and Wilkins' data, along with other information about the chemical properties of DNA, to build models of the molecule. They eventually proposed that the DNA molecule was a double helix, with the two strands of the helix held together by hydrogen bonds between the bases on each strand. The bases, adenine (A), thymine (T), cytosine (C), and guanine (G) are the letters of the DNA language which code for genetic information. Watson and Crick's discovery was a major breakthrough in the field of genetics, as it provided a fundamental understanding of how genetic information is stored and passed on from one generation to the next. It also paved the way for many future discoveries in the field of molecular biology, including the discovery of the genetic code, the structure of RNA and the mechanisms of DNA replication and protein synthesis. The discovery of the structure of DNA was a major milestone in the field of genetics and biology as it answered one of the biggest questions of that time: How does the genetic information of living organisms pass on to the next generations? This discovery was not only a scientific breakthrough but also a technological one as it opened the door to new methods of genetic engineering and biotechnology. Watson and Crick's discovery was also groundbreaking as it helped to explain how genetic diseases occur and how to treat them. It also helped to understand the evolution of living organisms and the diversity of life on Earth. Watson and Crick's discovery was awarded the Nobel Prize in Physiology or Medicine in 1962, along with Maurice Wilkins. Tragically Rosalind Franklin, who had provided key data for the discovery, died in 1958 at the age of 37. She was not included in the Nobel Prize as the rules state it cannot be awarded posthumously. Her major contribution was never fully acknowledged during that time, and it is only in recent years that this wrong has been corrected. The discovery of the double helix structure of DNA is considered one of the most important discoveries of the 20th century and has opened up a new era of research and development in the fields of genetics, medicine and biotechnology. It has also been crucial in solving many crimes with DNA evidence being crucial in catching criminals, sometimes years after the event. Human DNA sequences differ by 0.01 percent, meaning that there is very little on which to base distinctions between people. Professor Alec Jeffreys first used genetic profiling alongside the Forensic Science Service in 1983 to identify DNA from 5,000 volunteers during a murder investigation. Officials delivered blood and saliva samples to his lab at the University of Leicester, where it underwent pattern recognition. The samples helped exonerate one man who had confessed to the crime during the investigation. The DNA also helped identify local baker, Colin Pitchfork, as the perpetrator of the murders.

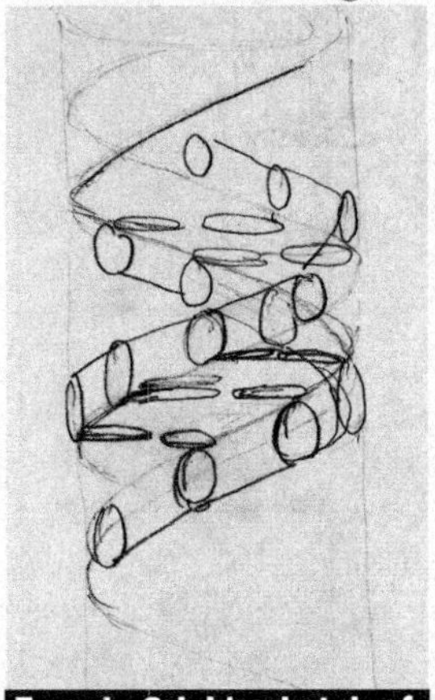
Francis Crick's sketch of the double helix

The Conviction of Derek Bentley

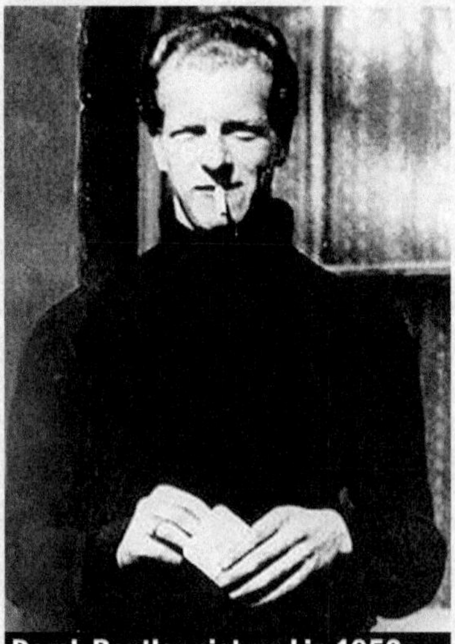

Derek Bentley pictured in 1952

Derek Bentley was a young man from London, who was convicted and hanged for the murder of a police officer in 1953. The case gained widespread attention and controversy due to questions surrounding Bentley's guilt and the fairness of his trial. The incident occurred on 2nd November 1952, when Bentley and his accomplice, Christopher Craig, attempted to break into a warehouse. The police were called and a confrontation ensued in which Craig shot and killed police officer Sidney Miles. Bentley was also present at the scene, but there was debate about whether he had actively participated and whether he had encouraged Craig to shoot the officer. Bentley was arrested and charged with murder, despite witnesses stating that he had not taken part in the shooting. At his trial, Bentley claimed that he had not had any intention of committing a crime and that he had been under Craig's influence. However, the prosecution argued that Bentley had encouraged Craig to shoot the officer and had thus played a crucial role in the crime. Bentley was found guilty of murder and sentenced to death, despite the fact that at the time of the crime, he was only 19 years old and had a mental age of 11. Craig, who had actually fired the shots, was too young to be sentenced to death. Bentley's case caused widespread public outrage and calls for clemency. Many people believed that he was not guilty of murder and that he had been unfairly tried. Despite appeals for clemency, Bentley was hanged on 28th January 1953. The case of Derek Bentley had a significant impact on the British legal system. It led to changes in the way that suspects were questioned by the police and the way that trials were conducted. It also contributed to the eventual abolition of the death penalty in the United Kingdom. In 1991, a film was made with Christopher Eccleston playing the part of Derek Bentley. The film's title *Let Him Have It* is taken from the words Bentley was heard to utter, just before the shooting. At the time the jury took those words to mean an instruction to Craig to shoot the officer. But doubt was cast as the phrase could also have been an instruction to Craig to surrender his gun. In 1998, the Court of Appeal quashed Derek Bentley's conviction, acknowledging that the then legal direction to the jury was flawed and that Bentley's conviction was 'unsafe'. This case was a significant example of the issues surrounding the death penalty, the fairness of trials and the treatment of those with mental disabilities in the legal system. It also highlighted the importance of proper legal representation and the need for a fair and just legal system. Craig, who was aged 16 and too young to be hanged, was ordered to be detained at Her Majesty's pleasure and was released in 1963 after serving 10 years' imprisonment.

Bentley was executed at HM Wandsworth prison

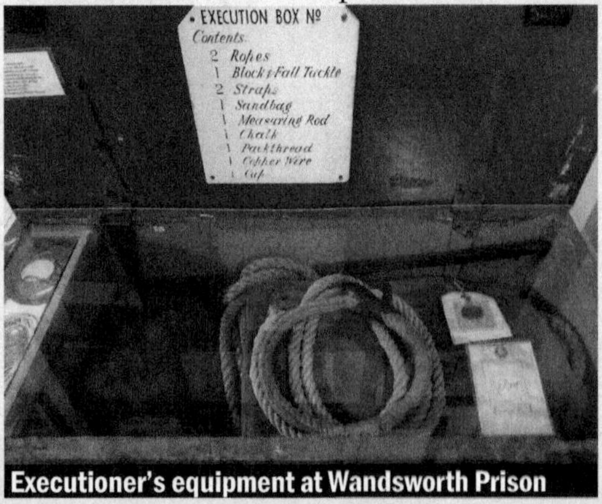

Executioner's equipment at Wandsworth Prison

The George Cross | The Highest Civilian Award for Bravery

David Broadfoot GC
credit: vconline.org.uk

David Broadfoot GC (21st July 1899 - 31st January 1953) was a Scottish seaman awarded the George Cross for his bravery during the sinking of the Princess Victoria. He was born in Stranraer, Scotland. In 1917 aged 18, he had gained a radio licence and later qualified as a ship's Radio Officer. In this capacity, he served in the merchant navy during both world wars. In October 1950, he joined the crew of the Merchant vessel *Princess Victoria*. He was serving on board the ship on 31st January 1953, when it sank in the North Channel, between Scotland and Northern Ireland, in the worst maritime disaster in United Kingdom waters since World War II. The *SS Princess Victoria* left Stranraer on the morning of 31st January, 1953, carrying 127 passengers for Larne. After leaving Loch Ryan she encountered north-westerly gales and squalls of sleet and snow. A heavy sea struck the ship and burst open the stern doors and sea water flooded the space on the car deck causing a list to starboard of about 10 degrees. Attempts were made to secure the stern doors but without success. The Master tried to steer his ship back to Loch Ryan but the conditions were of such severity that the manoeuvre failed. Some of the ship's cargo shifted from the port to the starboard side and this increased the list as the crippled vessel endeavoured to make her way across the Irish Sea. From the moment when *Princess Victoria* first got into difficulties, Radio Officer Broadfoot sent out wireless messages giving the ship's position and asking for assistance. The severe list which the vessel had taken, and which was gradually increasing, rendered his task even more difficult. Despite the difficulties and danger, he steadfastly continued his work at the transmitting set, repeatedly sending signals to the coastal radio station to enable them to ascertain the ship's exact position. When *Princess Victoria* finally stopped in sight of the Irish Coast her list had increased to 45 degrees. The vessel was practically on her beam ends and the order to abandon ship was given. Thinking only of saving the lives of passengers and crew, Radio Officer Broadfoot remained in the W/T cabin, receiving and sending messages, although he must have known that if he did this he had no chance of surviving. The ship finally foundered and Radio Officer Broadfoot went down with her. He had deliberately sacrificed his own life in an attempt to save others. He was posthumously awarded the George Cross, the highest award for bravery given to British civilians. In 1999, his grandchildren donated the George Cross to the Stranraer town museum, where it is now on display along with other memorabilia from the sinking.

SS Princess Victoria (credit: vconline.org.uk)

His gravestone is in the Inch Parish Churchyard in Inch, Scotland; several memorials of the disaster are located on both sides of the North Channel.

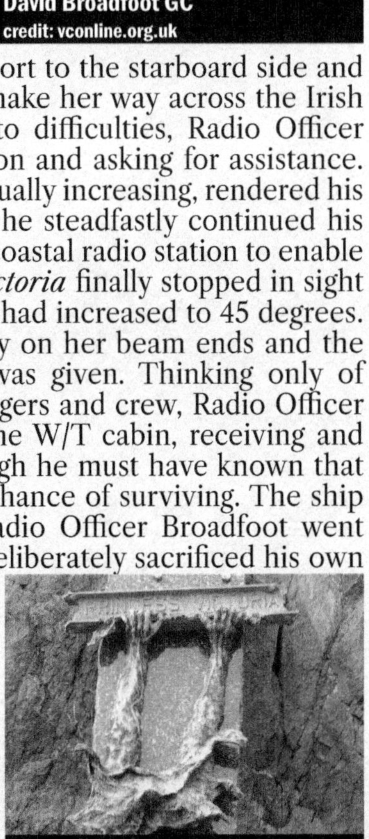

Memorial in Portpatrick

The Piltdown Man

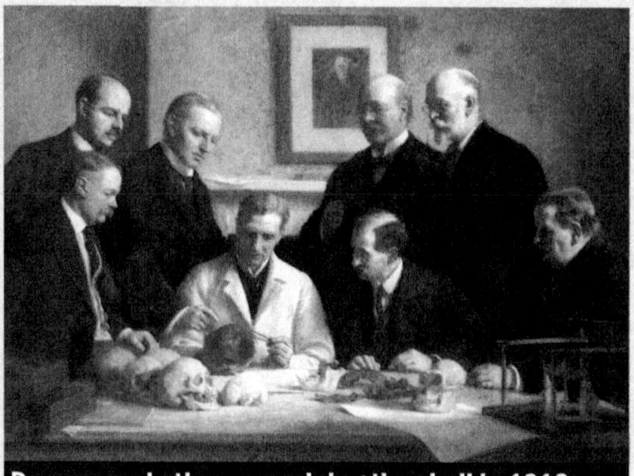

Dawson and others examining the skull in 1912

The Piltdown Man hoax was a scientific fraud perpetrated in the early 20th century. In 1912, Charles Dawson, an amateur archaeologist and lawyer, announced that he had found the fossilised remains of an early human ancestor in a gravel pit in Piltdown, East Sussex. The discovery, which he named Eoanthropus dawsoni (Dawson's Dawn Man), was hailed as a major breakthrough in the field of human evolution. The Piltdown Man was said to be a missing link between apes and humans, with a skull that combined the characteristics of both. The skull was large and had a brain capacity similar to that of modern humans, while the jaw and teeth were more apelike. The discovery was widely accepted by the scientific community and was used as evidence for human evolution for over 40 years. However, in 1953, scientists at the British Natural History Museum re-examined the Piltdown Man fossils and discovered that they were a forgery. The skull was found to be a composite of a human skull and the jaw of an orangutan, which had been artificially worn down and stained to make them appear ancient. The teeth had also been filed down to give them a human like appearance. The Piltdown Man hoax was a major embarrassment for the scientific community and led to a loss of credibility for the field of palaeoanthropology. It also had a significant impact on the study of human evolution, as the Piltdown Man had been used as a key piece of evidence for the "missing link" theory. The identity of the person or group behind the hoax has never been conclusively proven, but Charles Dawson is the main suspect. Some scientists believe that he may have perpetrated the hoax alone or may himself have been duped into believing the fraud, while others think he may have had accomplices. Dawson died in 1916, so he was never able to confirm or deny the allegations. The Piltdown Man hoax serves as a reminder of the importance of scepticism and critical thinking in the scientific process. It is also important to note that the Piltdown Man hoax had real-world consequences, as it influenced the way scientists thought about human evolution for decades. The idea of a 'missing link' between apes and humans was widely accepted and the Piltdown Man was used as evidence to support this theory. This led to a focus on finding a single missing link, rather than considering the complexity and diversity of human evolution. Additionally, the hoax also had implications for the study of human origins in Africa. At the time, the idea of Africa as the birthplace of humankind was not widely accepted and many scientists were searching for the origins of humanity in Europe. The discovery of the Piltdown Man seemed to support this idea. It took many years for the true importance of Africa in human evolution to be recognised. The story also highlights the potential for bias and the impact that such bias can have on the interpretation of data and the advancement of knowledge. A 2003 university study revealed 38 specimens in Dawson's antiquarian collection to be fakes.

A 1913 reconstruction

The Waco Tornadoes

The ALICO building left standing

On 11th May 1953, a series of tornadoes swept through the city of Waco, Texas causing significant destruction and loss of life. The most devastating of these tornadoes, rated as an F5 on the Fujita scale, the highest rating struck the city at around 7:00 PM local time. The tornado had wind speeds estimated at more than 260 miles per hour. It carved a path of destruction that was over a mile wide and several miles long. The tornado hit the city without warning, and many residents were caught off guard. It struck the downtown area first, destroying a number of buildings and injuring dozens of people. As the tornado moved eastward, it destroyed homes, businesses and schools, leaving a trail of destruction in its wake. The death toll from the Waco tornadoes was 114 people, with 597 people injured. Many of the fatalities occurred in the downtown area where the tornado hit with the greatest force. The destruction was widespread, with over 600 homes and buildings destroyed and another 1,000 damaged. The cost of the damage was estimated at more than $41 million. The Waco tornadoes were among the deadliest and most destructive in US history and serve as a tragic reminder of the power of nature. The city was left reeling in the aftermath of the disaster as residents struggled to come to terms with the loss of life and property. The response from local, state and federal government was quick and efficient, with search and rescue teams, medical personnel and emergency crews arriving on the scene within hours of the disaster. The Red Cross, The Salvation Army and other relief organisations also provided aid to the victims. The local government declared a state of emergency and the governor of Texas, Allan Shivers, arrived in Waco the following day to survey the damage. The disaster prompted a review of the city's tornado warning system, which was found to be inadequate. The city of Waco installed new warning sirens and improved its communication systems to ensure that residents would be better prepared in the event of another tornado. In the aftermath of the disaster, the city rallied together to rebuild and recover. The Waco community came together to support each other and to help those who had been affected by the disaster. The event served as a reminder of the importance of being prepared for natural disasters and it prompted many communities across the United States to take steps to improve their emergency response systems. 1953 was a particularly deadly tornado season in the USA. In total more than 400 people lost their lives and thousands more lost their livelihoods across the mid-west of the United States.

Buildings were reduced to rubble

A memorial plaque in Waco

The Great Kefalonia Earthquake

The Ionian earthquake of 1953 was a devastating event that struck the Greek island of Kefalonia on 12th August 1953. The magnitude 7.2 earthquake caused widespread damage, destroying much of the island's infrastructure and killing around 600 people. It struck in the early morning when most people were asleep in their homes. This contributed to the high death toll. Many buildings were completely destroyed and the damage was further exacerbated by aftershocks that continued to hit the area over the following days and weeks. The Royal Navy vessels *HMS Gambia* and *HMS Bermuda* were among the first on the scene to offer assistance to the islanders. Four vessels from Israel also responded to the calls for help. The earthquake had a profound impact on the island's economy, as the damage to infrastructure and buildings affected many businesses and left many people without a source of income. The Greek government and international aid organisations quickly mobilised to provide relief efforts and assist with rebuilding efforts. Despite these efforts, the island of Kefalonia was never fully able to recover from the effects of the earthquake. Many people were forced to leave their homes and migrate to other parts of Greece or abroad to the UK, South Africa, Canada and America in search of work and a normal life. In 1953 the island had a population of 120,000 and although it has recovered somewhat, it is still now under 40,000. Many of its towns were simply abandoned and these ghost towns are now advertised as ghoulish tourist attractions. The impact of the earthquake on the island's population and economy was felt for decades. In the aftermath, there was a push for improved building codes and earthquake preparedness in Greece. The tragedy of the Ionian earthquake led to increased awareness of the importance of disaster planning with the Greek government making efforts to improve its response to future disasters. This catastrophic event changed the way seismologists and the wider scientific community measured the impact of natural disasters. For example, Hurricane Katrina, which struck the coast of the Southern United States on 30th August 2005 killed 1,833 people, but it also displaced 1.2 million Louisianans. The increase in poverty with it lower life expectancy, and the higher rates of suicide associated with stress and loss of income put the death toll much higher.

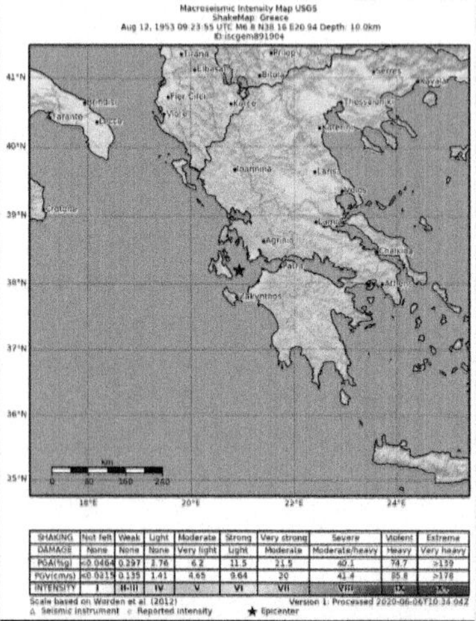

The star shows the epicentre

Nearly every building on the island was destroyed

The devastation viewed from a US Air Force plane

The North Sea Flood of 1953

Tens of thousands of buildings were destroyed

The 1953 North Sea flood was a devastating natural disaster that affected the coastal regions of the Netherlands, Belgium, England and Scotland on the 31st January 1953. It was caused by a combination of a high spring tide and a severe storm surge, which led to the breaching of sea defences and flooding of low-lying areas. In England, the flood affected the counties of Kent and Essex, claiming the lives of 307 people. Canvey Island, Jaywick and Burnham-on-Crouch were particularly badly affected, with many homes being destroyed or badly damaged. A poor warning system compounded the disaster. In Scotland, the flood affected the coastal towns of Montrose and Stonehaven, but the damage was relatively minor compared to the other affected areas. Warning telephone calls that were relayed down the coast went largely unanswered. In the Netherlands, the flood claimed the lives of 1,835 people and left 70,000 homeless. The provinces of Zeeland and South Holland were hardest hit, with the city of Dordrecht bearing the brunt. The flooding caused extensive damage to infrastructure, including roads, railways and buildings. Many dykes were breached and large areas of land were flooded. The Dutch government declared a state of emergency and the military was deployed to assist with evacuations and relief efforts. In Belgium, the flood claimed the lives of 31 people and caused significant damage to the coastal regions of West Flanders and East Flanders. The city of Ostend was particularly hard hit, with large areas of the city being flooded. The 1953 North Sea flood was one of the worst natural disasters in the history of the Low Countries and it had a significant impact on the lives of those affected. The disaster led to a renewed focus on sea defence flood protection measures and early warning systems. Many of the lessons learned from the flood were applied in the construction of the Delta Works in the Netherlands, which were completed in 1997. The disaster also led to the creation of the International Commission for the Protection of the North Sea, which was established to coordinate the efforts of the countries in the region to protect against future flooding. There were several individual acts of heroism during the disaster. Fred Sadd, a firefighter, is credited with saving 27 people in Gorleston-on-Sea in Norfolk. Mr Sadd, who lived in nearby Caister-on-Sea, plunged into the choppy waters, with no regard for his own safety and carried families away from Bells Marsh Road on his back and shoulders. He was awarded the George Medal by Queen Elizabeth II, and also the Exemplary Fire Service Medal and the Defence Medal. His medals went on display at Great Yarmouth Town Hall on 31st January 2023, the seventieth anniversary of the flood and his remarkable acts of bravery.

Defences were breached with devastating consequences

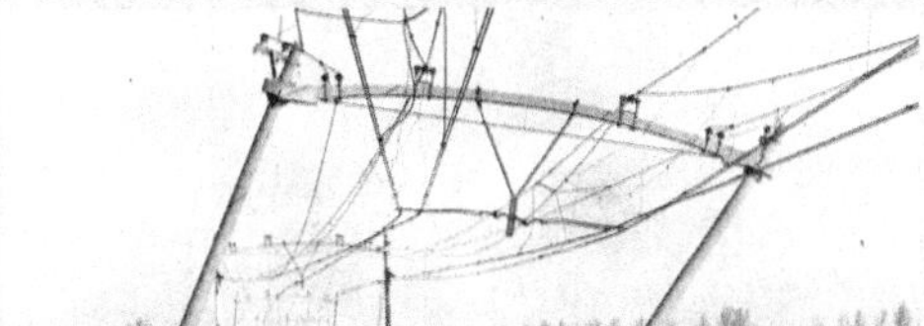
Train line infrastructure was wrecked

The 'Matthews' FA Cup Final | 2nd May 1953

Stanley Matthews

It will forever be remembered as the "Matthews Final". Blackpool 4-3 Bolton Wanderers. Stanley Matthews, the first ever Football Writers' Association Footballer of the Year in 1948, was the most popular player of his generation. More Bobby Charlton than David Beckham in his appeal, he had twice been on the losing side in FA Cup finals with Blackpool (aka The Seasiders) in 1948 and 1951. At 38, the clock was ticking; could the man nicknamed the *Wizard of the Dribble* make it third time lucky? Nat Lofthouse, the great Bolton and England centre-forward, conceded: "Everybody in England, except the people of Bolton, wanted Stanley to get his medal. We had a huge emotional barrier to break down." The country had its wish, but was it really the Matthews Final? Did the emotions of the nation and the media create an image that was more fantasy than reality? Stan Mortensen scored a hat-trick and Bill Perry netted the dramatic late winner. Even Matthews was heard to say: "To be honest, I found the whole thing one big embarrassment. Every time I hear the words Matthews' Final, I cringe with embarrassment because quite simply it's not true." Queen Elizabeth II was present at the final and she was clearly impressed as Matthews became the only player to have been knighted while still playing football.

Matthews' jersey for the final

England Vs Hungary | 25th November 1953

Ferenc Puskás

The 1953 match between England and Hungary at Wembley Stadium in London, which became known as the "Match of the Century," was an historic event in the world of football. England was seen as the dominant footballing nation at the time, but Hungary's impressive form leading up to the match suggested that they would be a strong opponent. The match itself was a stunning upset, as Hungary won 6-3 in what was England's first ever home defeat to a team from outside of the British Isles. The Hungarian team, led by legendary forward Ferenc Puskás, completely outplayed England with Puskás scoring twice and Nándor Hidegkuti also scoring two goals. The match was notable for Hungary's innovative 'Magical Magyars' playing style, which was based on fluid, attacking football and quick, short passing. This style of play was a revelation for English football, which was still rooted in a more traditional, direct approach. The match was a turning point in the history of English football and is widely regarded as one of the most important matches ever. It led to a rethinking of the way English football was played, and prompted a revolution in tactics and coaching that transformed the sport in the country. Lessons were learned, particularly by the right back, one Alf Ramsey, who would incorporate the Hungarian tactics and methods into his own approach, which would ultimately lead to England's triumph at the 1966 World Cup.

1953 Wimbledon Women's Singles Final

Maureen Connolly (USA) beat Doris Hart (USA) 8-6 7-5

Maureen Connolly

Maureen Connolly, also known as 'Little Mo', was an American tennis player born on 17th September 1934, in San Diego, California. She began playing tennis at a young age and quickly showed a natural talent for the sport. In 1951, at the age of 16, Connolly won her first major tournament, the US National Championships. She went on to win the US Nationals for the next two years, becoming the youngest player to win three consecutive titles. In 1953, she won Australian, French, Wimbledon and US Championships, completing a calendar-year Grand Slam. Connolly was known for her powerful forehand and her aggressive style of play. She was also known for her mental toughness and her ability to come back from behind. Her career was cut short in 1954 when she was involved in a riding accident that severely injured her right leg. Despite several surgeries, she was unable to play tennis again. In her short career, Connolly won a total of 9 Grand Slam titles and was ranked the world No. 1 player for three consecutive years. She was inducted into the International Tennis Hall of Fame in 1968. Connolly's legacy in the sport of tennis continues to be celebrated, and she is remembered as one of the greatest female players of all time.

Hart and Connolly on court

1953 Australian Open Men's Singles Final

Ken Rosewall (AUS) beat Mervyn Rose (AUS) 6-0 6-3 6-4

Australian Ken Rosewall

Ken Rosewall is an Australian tennis legend who is widely regarded as one of the greatest players in the history of the sport. He was born on 2nd November 1934, in Sydney, Australia, and began playing tennis at a young age. Rosewall's career spanned from the 1950s to the 1970s and during that time, he won a total of 8 Grand Slam singles titles. He won his first Grand Slam singles title at the Australian Championships in 1953 when he was just 18 years old. In singles he went on to win the Australian Championships three more times, the French Championships twice and the US National twice. Wimbledon was the one singles grand slam tournament that eluded him; he was beaten in the final four times between 1954 and 1974. Rosewall was known for his elegant and versatile playing style, which allowed him to excel on any surface. He was particularly known for his exceptional backhand and his ability to play a variety of shots with great accuracy and consistency. He made up for being relatively small in stature with his agility and quick reflexes, which helped him to cover the court effectively. He was also a successful doubles player winning a career Grand Slam.

Rugby Union 1953 | Wales vs New Zealand

Wales captain Bleddyn Williams

For every Welsh rugby fan and probably many New Zealanders too, the 19th December 1953 is a date forever etched in the memory. Why? Because it was the last time Wales beat the All Blacks in a Test match. Since that memorable day in Cardiff, Wales have tried and ultimately failed, many times against the 'Men in Black'. One of rugby's greatest rivalries hence became of the most one-sided in sport. Back in the Queen's coronation year, though, Wales versus New Zealand was one of the most eagerly anticipated sporting clashes. Still reeling from a defeat by club side Cardiff earlier in the week, the tourists were welcomed by a crowd of 56,000 at Cardiff Arms Park. While Welsh people will wonder whether they will ever witness Wales beating New Zealand in their lifetime, Cardiff rugby club and country captain Bleddyn Williams managed it twice in four days. Wales trailed 8-5 in the last 15 minutes, with wing Gareth Griffiths playing on with a dislocated shoulder and Williams having torn thigh ligaments. Then flanker Sid Judd crossed the try line to level the scores, At the time, tries were only awarded three points before the value increased to four in 1971. Soon after, Wales back-row forward Clem Thomas had the ball on the wing and caught the All Blacks flat-footed when he launched a diagonal kick over the New Zealand 25-yard-line. Wing Ken Jones, latched onto the loose ball to score the winning try to complete Wales' third victory in four meetings with New Zealand. Wales ran out 13-8 winners.

Rugby League 1953 | Huddersfield Vs St. Helens Rugby Challenge Cup Final

The Challenge Cup trophy

On the 25th April 1953 in front of a crowd of 89,400 Huddersfield met St. Helens at Wembley to contest the Rugby League Challenge Cup Final. St. Helens (aka The Saints) went in to the game as favourites. They were captained by Doug Greenall and featured the flying Welsh winger Steve Llewellyn. They would both be later inducted into the St. Helens Hall of Fame. Huddersfield started well and it was they who drew first blood. Peter Ramsden celebrated his 19th birthday with the first try of the game. St. Helens came roaring back with a try through Llewellyn and a further try and two goals from George Langfield. Huddersfield needed inspiration. It came in the shape of Billy Banks who went in for a cheeky try. Lionel Cooper converted. The game was now even with The Saints' forward pack dominating in the scrums and in turn possession. But Huddersfield's forwards had a determination in the loose, particularly Bowden, Slevin and Valentine. To end his fairy-tale day, Peter Ramsden managed to get on the end of a move engineered by Valentine and Bowden to score the winning try and won the Lance Todd Trophy for Man of the Match to cap a birthday he would never forget. Lionel Cooper added the conversion to make the final score Huddersfield 15-10 St. Helens, making Huddersfield Rugby League 1953 Challenge Cup Champions.

Cricket

It is the 15th August 1953, the first day of the fifth and final Test with England ready to burst. The nation had been waiting 27 years to celebrate Ashes success on home soil, with the frustration exacerbated by four draws in the build-up to the final meeting at The Oval. The match had been extended to six days in an attempt to guarantee a result. A full 24 hours before play got under way the queue for tickets formed outside; by evening it stretched around the ground. *The Sydney Morning Herald* previewed it as "the Test to end Tests". "Anyone who has ever fallen under the spell of cricket will insist to his dying day that it is the finest game in the world" they wrote. "Yet there are times when even its most loyal champions feel sensitive to criticism of the game, and it must be confessed that the present series of Test matches has left openings for the kind of ridicule which most annoys them. There is something a trifle absurd in the thought that the picked teams of Australia and England have now flung themselves at each other four times over a period of 20 days without so far achieving a single result. Today, however, all that will be forgotten. On this occasion one may feel that it matters very little which side wins provided that one of them does."

The Ashes Urn

Perhaps buoyed by the fervour of the Coronation, one team did win and it was England. Australia batted first; England took the iniativie as bowlers Fred Trueman and Alec Bedser ripped through the top order, before Australian bowler Ray Lindwall, batting at number 9, offered some resistance top-scoring with 62. England's response was positive with Len Hutton and Peter May sharing a second wicket century stand after the fall of opener Bill Edrich. Lindwall added to his batting heroics by removing much of England's middle order before England reached a score of 309, thanks in no small part to a contribution of 62 from Trevor 'Barnacle' Bailey. They went into the second innings leading by 31 runs. In Australia's second innings the spin duo of Tony Lock and Jim Laker bamboozled the tourists, sharing nine of the ten wickets between them (the other was a run out). England were set a small target. After an initial fright when captain Len Hutton was run out for 17, Edrich, May and Compton guided the home side to victory, finishing on 132/2. Bill Edrich top scored with a 55 not out. Elsewhere, Surrey won the County Championship and Neil Harvey, Tony Lock, Keith Miller, Johnny Wardle and Willie Watson, were named Wisden's cricketers of the year.

Len Hutton

Alec Bedser

Sir Gordon Richards and the 1953 Epsom Derby

Sir Gordon Richards, who was knighted in 1953 in recognition of his services to horse racing, was arguably the most successful flat jockey in British racing history. During an extraordinary career between 1921 and 1954, Richards rode a total of 4,870 winners and became champion jockey on 26 occasions. In 1947, Richards rode 269 winners thereby setting a British record that would stand for 55 years until it was beaten by the incomparable Sir Anthony McCoy. Richards also enjoyed considerable success in British classic races winning The St. Leger five times, The 2,000 Guineas three times, The 1,000 Guineas three times and The Oaks twice. However, for much of his career the most important classic of all, the Derby, proved elusive. In fact, it was not until the so-called 'Coronation' Derby of 1953, run just five days after he had been knighted that Richards broke his duck in the Epsom classic. On that occasion, he rode the 5/1 joint-favourite, Pinza, owned by Sir Victor Sassoon and trained by Norman Bertie. Shikampur, owned by the Aga Khan, led the field into the final quarter of a mile. However, he was caught by Pinza, who drew away in the closing stages to win by four lengths. Aureole, owned by the Queen, came around the outside of the field to finish second, but was always in vain pursuit. Richards would retire the following year, but not before one of the most controversial incidents in British horse racing...

Pinza with Gordon Richards (inset)
with thanks to John Slusar, www.greyhoundderby.com

Sir Gordon Richards as depicted on a Gallaher's cigarette card

In 1954 Lester Piggott's first Derby winner Never Say Die also appeared in the King Edward VII Stakes at Royal Ascot, which is where things turned ugly. Never Say Die was second favourite to the Derby runner-up and market leader Arabian Night who had an 8lb pull (weight advantage). However Piggott was still strongly fancied to add the 'Ascot Derby' to his Epsom laurels. It was a very rough race, a great deal happening in the short home straight. As the field turned for home, with Blue Prince II and Arabian Night leading the way, those behind prepared to deliver their challenges. Sir Gordon Richards, riding Rashleigh, came round the bend with two horses between him and the rail: Garter (ridden by Lester's cousin Bill Rickaby) and Dragon Fly (Doug Smith). Lester and Never Say Die were just behind. The race ended in a melee with Richards' mount winning and Piggott's finishing fourth. The stewards held an inquiry and initially blamed Richards, but the senior jockeys closed ranks and testified against Piggott. They stripped Lester of his licence and set no time limit on his sentence, suggesting he might consider reapplying after six months. Furthermore, in an act of astonishingly petty vindictiveness, he was also required to leave home and work away from his father Keith's yard. The verdict was received by Lester with barely concealed fury and also by the racing public with vociferous outrage. Piggott was allowed to return to the saddle some time later, but only after Richards had retired.

Lester Piggott

Sir Stirling Moss

Sir Stirling Moss (1929-2020) was a legendary British racing driver, widely considered one of the greatest drivers of all time. He competed in Formula One, sports cars and touring cars, and achieved numerous victories and podium finishes during his career. Moss made his debut in Formula One in 1951, driving for the Hersham and Walton Motors (HWM) team. He quickly gained a reputation as a skilled and fearless driver, known for his ability to push his car to the limit while still maintaining control. He went on to race for a number of teams, including Maserati, Mercedes-Benz and Lotus, and won a total of 16 Grand Prix races during his career.

Sir Stirling Moss (pictured in 1958)

1953 saw Moss at the pinnacle of his career. He won the Daily Express International Trophy for Production Touring Cars and the 12 Heures Internationales de Reims, both driving Jaguars, and the RAC British Grand Prix 500cc driving a Cooper-Norton MKVII. The one that got away was the Le Mans 24hr Race, where his and Peter Walker's Jaguar could only finish second to fellow Brits Tony Rolt and Duncan Hamilton also driving a Jaguar.

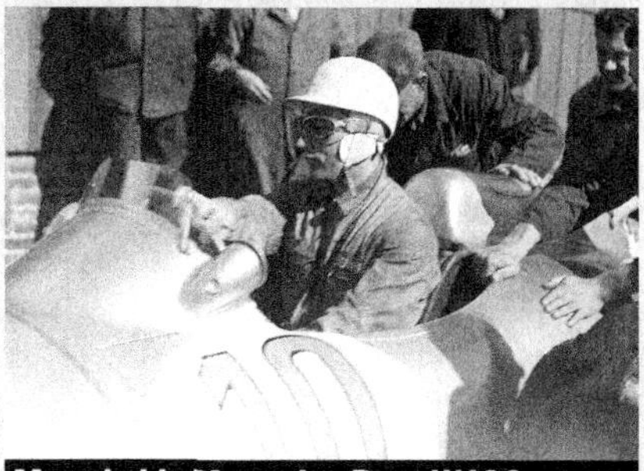
Moss in his Mercedes Benz W196

One of Moss's most famous victories came at the 1955 Mille Miglia, a gruelling 1,000-mile race through the streets of Italy. Driving a Mercedes-Benz 300 SLR, Moss set a record time of 10 hours, 7 minutes, and 48 seconds, a feat that many consider to be one of the greatest achievements in the history of motor sport.

Moss driving in the 1955 Mille Miglia

Moss retired from racing in 1962, after suffering a serious accident at Goodwood that left him in a coma for a month. Despite his retirement, he remained a revered figure in the racing world, and was known for his charm, wit and gentlemanly demeanour.

In recognition of his contributions to motor sport, Moss was awarded a knighthood in 2000. He passed away in 2020 at the age of 90, leaving behind a legacy as one of the greatest drivers of all time. For many years during and after his career, the rhetorical phrase "Who do you think you are, Stirling Moss?" was supposedly the standard question all British policemen asked speeding motorists. Moss related that he himself was once stopped for speeding and asked just that; he stated that the traffic officer had some difficulty believing him.

Moss victorious in the 1955 Mille Miglia alongside navigator Denis Jenkinson

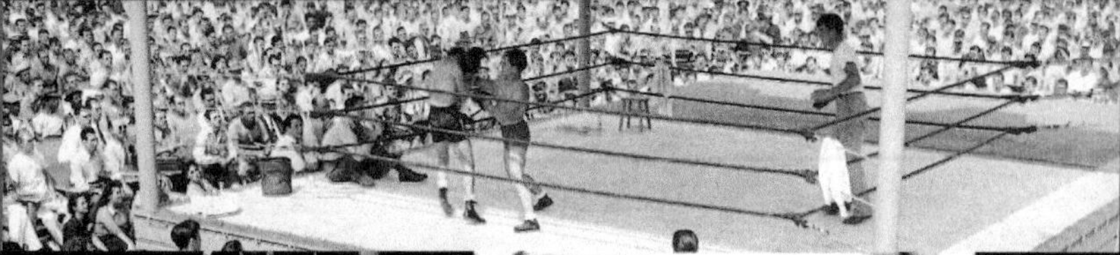

Rocky Marciano vs Jersey Joe Walcott

Rocky Marciano

The fight between Rocky Marciano and Jersey Joe Walcott was one of the most eagerly anticipated heavyweight boxing matches of the 1950s. It took place on the 23rd September 1953 in Philadelphia, Pennsylvania. Walcott, the challenger, was a former heavyweight champion who had held the title for two years before losing it to Ezzard Charles. He was looking to regain the title and become the first man to win the heavyweight championship three times. Marciano, the reigning heavyweight champion, was known for his heavy punching power and unrelenting style. He was undefeated in 42 professional fights, with 39 wins by knockout. The two fighters had different styles, with Walcott relying on his speed and footwork to avoid Marciano's punches, while Marciano used his powerful punches and relentless pressure to wear down his opponents. The fight was a back-and-forth battle, with both fighters exchanging blows throughout the first 12 rounds. In the 13th, Marciano delivered a devastating right hand to Walcott's jaw, knocking him out and retaining his heavyweight championship title. The knockout was one of the most memorable moments in heavyweight boxing history and cemented Marciano's legacy as one of the greatest heavyweight champions of all time. Marciano remains the only fighter to have stopped every opponent he ever faced for the world heavyweight title and shares, with Joe Louis, the highest knockout to-win percentage in world heavyweight title fights at 85.71%.

The Battle of Baroness Summerskill

Baroness Summerskill

Boxing was a participation sport, taught to boys in British state schools in 1953. In 1962 it stopped. It wasn't banned; it was just no longer fashionable. If you wanted to box, you then had to join a boxing club. Boxing was never outlawed in British schools, despite the best efforts of a physician and Labour MP, Edith Summerskill. Her anti-boxing campaign in the fifties won widespread support but lost several votes in the House of Commons. The votes may have gone against Summerskill, but the spirit of the age was with her all the way. The times were changing. Memories of the war were fading. National Service had ended. Boxing was falling out favour in the UK save for a minority of hardcore fans. Many people believed that boxing in schools was a relic of our more violent past. "Can anybody sensibly suggest that the screaming crowd round a boxing ring is having implanted in it the fine qualities of pluck, endurance and restraint? We are told by those in this business that the sole object in view is to give the spectators a display of a sport regulated by rules calculated to ensure the maximum enjoyment of boxing techniques. If that is so, why are these bouts accompanied in the newspapers and on the radio by a commentary deliberately phrased to emphasise the brutal element?"- *Dr. Edith Summerskill, Member for Warrington*.

The 1953 Open | 8th - 10th July

Ben Hogan made his only appearance in The Open in 1953 at Carnoustie and won the Claret Jug in a fitting climax to a glorious career. He was the greatest golfer of his generation. Since a car crash in 1949, in which he nearly died, he had played in very few tournaments, concentrating on the US Masters and the US Open. In 1953 he won both those titles and decided to make the journey to Scotland. He arrived a week early to practise with the smaller British ball and learn how to play the course. Just like everyone else, he had to qualify for The Open. When he did he produced rounds of 73, 71, 70 and 68 for a total of 282 and a four-stroke victory over Peter Thomson, Dai Rees, Antonio Cerda and amateur Frank Stranahan. He is one of only four Champion Golfers to improve his score each time over four rounds. Huge galleries followed his progress, his only other visit to Britain being for the 1956 Canada Cup at Wentworth. Struggles with his putter saw him post an opening round of 73, tied for seventh place, three shots behind fellow American Stranahan. Hogan continued to struggle on the greens in round two but a score of 71 moved him to a tie for fourth, on even par, as Scotland's Eric Brown and Wales' Dai Rees led the way on two-under, with Roberto De Vicenzo one stroke behind. In addition to the support of the locals, Hogan also had some famous fans in attendance as Frank Sinatra, who was performing at a concert in Dundee, was in the gallery for day two and told the media that "all America is rooting for Hogan". In the third round, the eight-time major winner made his move joining De Vicenzo atop the leader board after birdieing the 18th to card a 70. Battling chills, flu and old injuries from his car accident four years prior, Hogan later admitted he was desperate to avoid a 36-hole play-off. And he did in style. A remarkable birdie at the fifth changed the trajectory of his final round as he found himself deeply bunkered with a bad angle. He chipped in from 30 feet. He then birdied the par-five sixth by driving down the narrow alley of fairway between the bunkers and out of bounds on the left; a strip of land since known as Hogan's Alley. The soon-to-be champion then opened up a two-shot lead by the 13th, saved par at 17 and finished off a course record round of 68, bettering the mark set by Cerda in the third round earlier that morning, with a final birdie at the 18th. Not until Tiger Woods in 2000 would a player match his three major titles in the same year. It was the ninth and final major of Hogan's illustrious career, the last six coming in eight appearances. He vowed he would return but never did.

The 18th green at Carnoustie

Ben Hogan returning home in 1953

The British Open Claret Jug Trophy

On sale in the UK from 1953, the Austin-Healey 100 was a sports car built by a joint venture between the Austin division of the British Motor Corporation and the Donald Healey Motor Company. It was named for its ability to reach 100mph.

Hayley Earl, head of GM's styling group, noticed that GI's returning from overseas after the war were importing sports cars including MG's and Jaguars. He started a project to design an all-American sports car. The Corvette C1 was born.

The Westland Whirlwind helicopter first flew in 1953. It was based on the Sikorsky S-55/H-19 Chickasaw. They served with the Royal Navy's Fleet Air Arm for search and rescue until they were superseded by the Sea-King in the early 1970s.

The North American F-100 Super Sabre first flew on the 25th May 1953. It was the first USAF jet capable of supersonic speed in level flight. On 7th August 1959 two Super Sabre's became the first-ever jet fighters to fly over the North Pole.

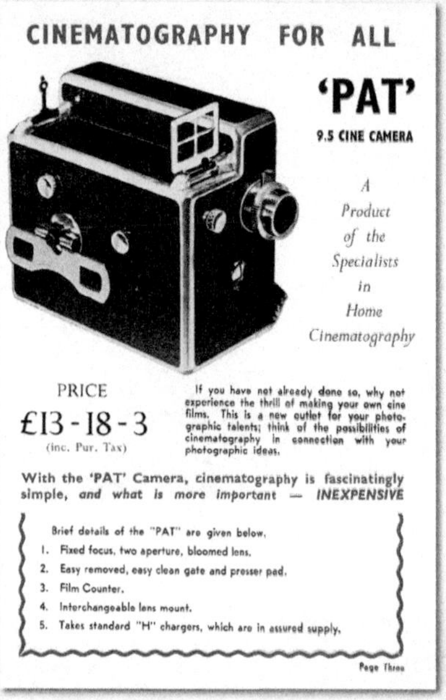

The British designed and built Pathéscope Pat was launched in 1953 as a low cost ciné camera. It was almost half the cost of its nearest competitor. It had a clockwork mechanism and used "H" film chargers.

The classic Rolex Submariner watch first went into production in 1953. Resistant to 100m water depth, the Submariner was the watch of choice for James Bond. Its massive popularity spurned many homage watches and illegal counterfeits.

Created in the early 1950's by the Swedish-Norwegian chocolate brand Marabou, the Daim Bar is a chocolate bar made from crunchy almond caramel covered in milk chocolate. It went on general sale in Sweden and Norway in 1953.

Originally launched in the USA under the brand name "Sugar Smacks" in 1953 by Kellogg's, the name later changed in the 1980s to "Honey Smacks". In the UK, the Quaker Oats Company launched the rival "Sugar Puffs" later in 1957.

Photo Credits

Credits shown in the order in which they appear in the book. Photos not listed are in the public domain.

Key to page numbers

fc = front cover; **ifc** = inside front cover; **tp** = title page; **cp** = contents page; **ap1** = acknowledgements page 1; **ap2** = acknowledgements page 2; **rop** = reader offer page; **ibc** = inside back cover; **bc** = back cover; **3** = page 3; **4** = page 4; etc.

Key to object position on page

tl = top left; *t* = top; *tc* = top centre; *tr* = top right; *cla* = centre left above; *ca* = centre above; *cra* = centre right above; *cl* = centre left; *c* = centre; *cr* = centre right; *clb* = centre left below; *cb* = centre below; *crb* = centre right below; *bl* = bottom left; *b* = bottom; *bc* = bottom centre; *br* = bottom right; *w* = whole page; *h* = header; *tb* = text background

Key to image licence types

CC BY-SA 2.0 = https://creativecommons.org/licenses/by-sa/2.0/deed.en;
CC BY-SA 3.0 = https://creativecommons.org/licenses/by-sa/3.0/deed.en;
CC BY-SA 4.0 = https://creativecommons.org/licenses/by-sa/4.0/deed.en;

(m) = image has been modified as permitted under licensing terms

fc *tl*: Walt Disney (m) © UCLA Library Special Collections, Wikimedia Commons, CC BY-SA 2.0; **fc** *crb*: Fireman changing points (m) © Archives New Zealand, Wikimedia Commons, CC BY-SA 2.0; **fc** *cla*: Palace Guard (m) © Sunshine34, Wikimedia Commons, CC BY-SA 3.0; **tp** *w*: Austin Healey (m) © Dan Smedley, Unsplash.com; **cp** *tl*: Prince Philip (m) © Archives New Zealand, Wikimedia Commons, CC BY-SA 2.0; **4** *cla*: Watson and Crick © Marjorie McCarty, Wikimedia Commons, CC BY-SA 2.5; **4** *clb*: Hillary and Norgay © Jamling Tenzing Norgay, Wikimedia Commons, CC BY-SA 2.0; **16** *cl*: Coronation Ceremony © BiblioArchives / LibraryArchives, Wikimedia Commons, CC BY-SA 2.0; **17** *cl*: Palace Balcony © BiblioArchives / LibraryArchives, Wikimedia Commons, CC BY-SA 2.0; **17** *cb*: Queen Elizabeth II waving © National Media Museum, Wikimedia Commons, CC BY-SA 2.0; **18** *cla*: Tony Blair © Pavel Golovkin, Wikimedia Commons, CC BY-SA 4.0; **19** *cla*: Victoria Wood © MAG (Mines Advisory Group), Wikimedia Commons, CC BY-SA 2.0; **19** *clb*: Michael Portillo © Smerus (David Conway), Wikimedia Commons, CC BY-SA 4.0; **20** *cla*: Kathleen Kennedy © Gage Skidmore, Wikimedia Commons, CC BY-SA 3.0; **20** *clb*: Benazir Bhutto © Oliver Mark, Wikimedia Commons, CC BY-SA 4.0; **21** *cla*: Cyndi Lauper © Philip Romano, Wikimedia Commons, CC BY-SA 4.0; **21** *clb*: Graham Gooch © fourthandfifteen, Wikimedia Commons, CC BY-SA 2.0; **22** *cla*: Nigel Mansell © Colin_Eric, Wikimedia Commons, CC BY-SA 2.0; **22** *clb*: Midge Ure © Drew de F Fawkes, Wikimedia Commons, CC BY-SA 2.0; **23** *cla*: Griff Rhys Jones © Phil Guest, Wikimedia Commons, CC BY-SA 2.0; **23** *clb*: Tina Brown © Financial Times, Wikimedia Commons, CC BY-SA 2.0; **24** *cla*: Franz Klammer © Manfred Werner / Tsui, Wikimedia Commons, CC BY-SA 3.0; **24** *clb*: John Malkovich © Petr Novák, Wikimedia Commons, CC BY-SA 3.0; **25** *cla*: Sir Trevor Phillips © Heinrich Böll Stiftung, Wikimedia Commons, CC BY-SA 2.0; **25** *clb row 1*: Nigel Planer © JN1550, Wikimedia Commons, CC BY-SA 3.0; **25** *cb row 1*: Michael Bolton © Gage Skidmore, Wikimedia Commons, CC BY-SA 3.0; **25** *crb row 1*: Isabelle Huppert © Georges Biard, Wikimedia Commons, CC BY-SA 4.0; **25** *cb row 2*: Rick Moranis © Alan Light, Wikimedia Commons, CC BY-SA 2.0; **25** *crb row 2*: Ruby Wax © Jjnoordman, Wikimedia Commons, CC BY-SA 4.0; **25** *clb row 3*: Sebastian Faulks © Elena Torre, Wikimedia Commons, CC BY-SA 2.0; **25** *cb row 3*: Mike Oldfield © Urmelbeauftragter, Wikimedia Commons, CC BY-SA 3.0; **25** *crb row 3*: Alfred Molina © Justin Hoch, Wikimedia Commons, CC BY-SA 2.0; **25** *clb row 4*: Tim Allen © MingleMediaTVNetwork, Wikimedia Commons, CC BY-SA 2.0; **25** *cb row 4*: Hulk Hogan © GabboT, Wikimedia Commons, CC BY-SA 2.0; **25** *crb row 4*: Roger Allem © Sonnenuntergang, Wikimedia Commons, CC BY-SA 3.0; **25** *clb row 5*: Kim Basinger © Alan Light, Wikimedia Commons, CC BY-SA 2.0; **25** *cb row 5*: Bill Pullman © greg2600, Wikimedia Commons, CC BY-SA 2.5; **25** *crb row 5*: Richard Clayderman © Mahalkita, Wikimedia Commons, CC BY-SA 3.0; **27** *cl*: Dylan Thomas © Jim Forest, Flickr.com, CC BY-SA 2.0; **29** *tl*: Coins © Jo Smiley Hailey, Unsplash.com; **29** *tr*: House © Sludgegulper, Wikimedia Commons, CC BY-SA 2.0; **29** *cl*: Morris Minor © SG2012, Wikimedia Commons, CC BY-SA 2.0; **29** *bl*: TV © Science Museum, Wikimedia Commons, CC BY-SA 4.0; **29** *bc*: Bread © Dmitry Makeev, Wikimedia Commons, CC BY-SA 4.0; **29** *br*: Petrol Station © Erik Mclean, Unsplash.com; **31** *tr*: Office © Huppertsberg, Wikimedia Commons, CC BY-SA 3.0; **37** *tr*: Lucienne Day © The Robin and Lucienne Day Foundation - Photographer: Studio Briggs, Wikimedia Commons, CC BY-SA 4.0; **38** *c*: Coronation Chicken © Brent Hofacker, Shutterstock.com; **39** *ca*: Cake © Kimberly Vardeman, Wikimedia Commons, CC BY-SA 2.0; **40** *tl*: Bikini Model © Harry Pot / Anefo, Wikimedia Commons, CC BY-SA 4.0; **40** *br*: Model © Jenny Freebairn; **41** *tl*: Seaside Models © Hans Pinn, Wikimedia Commons, CC BY-SA 3.0; **41** *tr*: Audrey Hepburn © Hans Gerber, Wikimedia Commons, CC BY-SA 4.0; **41** *bl*: Couple © daves_archive1, Flickr.com, CC BY-SA 2.0; **42** *tr*: Swimming Pool Model © Fritz Cohen, Flickr, CC BY-SA 3.0; **49** *tl*: Tokyo Story © Neonsigh, Wikimedia Commons, CC BY-SA 4.0; **50** *br*: Kids listening to radio © German Federal Archive, CC BY-SA 3.0; **51** *tl*: Andy Pandy © Chemical Engineer, CC BY-SA 3.0; **51** *clb*: All Your Own © BBC Archive; **52** *clb*: The Quatermass Experiment © BBC Archive; **53** *tl*: The Good Old Days © BBC Archive; **54** *bl*: Charlie Chaplin © Séeberger frères, Wikimedia Commons, CC BY-SA 1.0; **56** *tl*: The Beverley Sisters © Arxiu del So i de la Imatge de Mallorca, Flickr.com, CC BY-SA 2.0; **56** *cl* & **57** *clb*: Mantovani © Bert Verhoeff / Anefo, Wikimedia Commons, CC BY-SA 3.0; **56** *bl*: Eddie Calvert © Bradford Timeline, Wikimedia Commons, CC BY-SA 2.0; **60** *br*: Henry Moore © Allan warren, Wikimedia Commons, CC BY-SA 3.0; **61** *tl*: Gambling Chips © 18percentgrey, Adobe Stock; **61** *cl* & **61** *bl* & **62** *tl* & **62** *cl* & **62** *bl* & **63** *tl* & **63** *cl* & **63** *bl*: original artwork created with the assistance of AI using Dall-E2 and Stable Diffusion; **64** *bl*: The Crucible (m) © Len Radin, Flickr.com, CC BY-SA 2.0; **65** *tr*: Meeting The Queen © AndyCBaer, Wikimedia Commons, CC BY-SA 4.0; **65** *bl*: Jimmy Edwards © CHRIS SHAW, Wikimedia Commons, CC BY-SA 3.0; **66** *tr*: Reclining Figure © Andrew Dunn, Wikimedia Commons, CC BY-SA 2.0; **66** *cra*: Single Form © Andy Scott, Wikimedia Commons, CC BY-SA 4.0; **66** *crb*: Draped Reclining Woman © Rufus46, Wikimedia Commons, CC BY-SA 3.0; **67** *br*: Carol Ann Duffy © walnut whippet, Wikimedia Commons, CC BY-SA 2.0; **70** *tl*: DNA © Zephyris, Wikimedia Commons, CC BY-SA 3.0; **71** *bl*: Spike Waves © Der Lange, Wikimedia Commons, CC BY-SA 2.0; **73** *bl*: Coronation Coach © Eileen Warren, geograph.org.uk, CC BY-SA 2.0; **74** *tr*: Mount Everest © Vyacheslav Argenberg, Wikimedia Commons, CC BY-SA 4.0; **74** *clb*: Hillary and Norgay © Jamling Tenzing Norgay, Wikimedia Commons, CC BY-SA 2.0; **75** *tr*: Watson and Crick © Marjorie McCarty, Wikimedia Commons, CC BY-SA 2.5; **75** *clb*: DNA Sketch © Wellcome Images, Wikimedia Commons, CC BY-SA 4.0; **76** *tr*: Derek Bentley © PA Images / Alamy Stock Photo; **76** *cl*: Wandsworth Prison © Derek Harper, Wikimedia Commons, CC BY-SA 2.0; **76** *bl*: Execution Box © SchroCat, Wikimedia Commons, CC BY-SA 4.0; *continued on next page...*

Photo Credits continued

77 *tr*: David Broadfoot © vconline.org.uk; **77** *clb*: SS Princess Victoria © vconline.org.uk; **77** *br*: Memorial © I Craig, Wikimedia Commons, CC BY-SA 2.0; **79** *br*: Waco Memorial © Billy Hathorn, Wikimedia Commons, CC BY-SA 3.0; **80** *cl*: Destroyed Building © לת לארא המלש ףולא ביבא, Wikimedia Commons, CC BY-SA 3.0; **81** *tr* & **81** *cl*: Flood Pictures © Dutch National Archives, Wikimedia Commons, CC BY-SA 2.0; **81** *br*: Man Carrying Bike © Anefo / Dutch National Archives, Wikimedia Commons, CC BY-SA 2.0; **82** *cla*: Stanley Matthews' Jersey © Ben Sutherland, Wikimedia Commons, CC BY-SA 2.0; **82** *br*: Puskás © FORTEPAN adományozó Magyar Bálint, Wikimedia Commons, CC BY-SA 3.0; **84** *br*: Trophy © Chemical Engineer, Wikimedia Commons, CC BY-SA 3.0; **84** *tr*: Ashes Urn © danielgreef/Dan, Wikimedia Commons, CC BY-SA 2.0; **86** *tr*: Pinza © John Slusar, greyhoundderby.com; **86** *br*: Lester Piggott © Ragge Strand, Bjørn Fjørtoft, Rolf Engesland, Wikimedia Commons, CC BY-SA 4.0; **89** *tr*: Carnoustie 18th Green (m) © Jim Smillie, Wikimedia Commons, CC BY-SA 2.0; **90** *t*: Austin Healey (m) © Sicnag, Wikimedia Commons, CC BY-SA 2.0; **91** *t*: Westland Whirlwind © Airwolfhound, Wikimedia Commons, CC BY-SA 2.0; **91** *b*: Super Sabre © US Air Force, Wikimedia Commons, CC BY-SA 4.0; **92** *b*: Rolex closeup © Mark Mathosian, Flickr.com, CC BY-SA 2.0; **89** *b*: Honey Smacks in bowl (m) © Th78blue, Wikimedia Commons, CC BY-SA 4.0; **89** *b*: Marble (m) © Yana Iskayeva, Unsplash.com; **96** *tc*: Coffee Table (m) © Sincerely Media, Unsplash.com; **BC** *tl*: Queen Elizabeth speaking (m) © Archives New Zealand, Wikimedia Commons, CC BY-SA 2.0; **BC** *tr*: Ann Baxter (m) © IISG, Wikimedia Commons, CC BY-SA 2.0;

Graphic and Background Image Credits

Credits shown in the order in which they appear in the book.

Additional Key

(ic) = icon; (ph) = photo

fc *c*, **tp** *ca*, **bc** *w* : (ph) Texture by Felipe Santana, Unsplash; **cp, 3-15**: (ph) Wood by Michael Schwarzenberger, Pixabay; **16-96** *tb*: (m)(ph) Paper Texture by rawpixel.com; **3** *cla*: (ic) Play by Adrien Coquet, thenounproject.com, CC BY-SA 2.0; **6,8,10,12,14** *tl* & **7,9,11,13,15** *tr*: (ic) Newspaper by Loic Poivet, thenounproject.com, CC BY-SA 2.0; **6-15** *c*: (ph) Book by Robert Armstrong, Pixabay; **18-27,44-67,90-96** *w*: (m)(ph) Concrete texture by rawpixel.com; **16,17** *w*: (ph) Westminster Abbey © Carlotta Benini, Wikimedia Commons, CC BY-SA 3.0; **16** *tl* & **17** *tr*: (ic) Royal Crown by Vectors Market, thenounproject.com, CC BY-SA 2.0; **18,20,22,24** *tl* & **19,21,23,25** *tr*: (ic) Birthday Calendar by Kiran Shastry, thenounproject.com, CC BY-SA 2.0; **18** *cla* & **19** *clb* & **20** *clb* & **26** *cla*: (ic) Speaker by popcornarts, thenounproject.com, CC BY-SA 2.0; **18,24** *clb* & **26** *cl* & **27** *cla*: (ic) Theatre by Ben Davis, thenounproject.com, CC BY-SA 2.0; **19,23** *cla*: (ic) Theatre Comedy by B Farias, thenounproject.com, CC BY-SA 2.0; **20** *cla*: (ic) Clapper Board by Andrew Nielsen, thenounproject.com, CC BY-SA 2.0; **21** *cla*: (ic) Microphone by andriwidodo, thenounproject.com, CC BY-SA 2.0; **21** *clb*: (ic) Cricket by SANB, thenounproject.com, CC BY-SA 2.0; **22** *cla*: (ic) Racing Helmet by ainul muttaqin, thenounproject.com, CC BY-SA 2.0; **22** *clb*: (ic) Music Note by Karen Tyler, thenounproject.com, CC BY-SA 2.0; **23** *clb*: (ic) Journalist by Maan Icons, thenounproject.com, CC BY-SA 2.0; **24** *cla*: (ic) Skier by Icons 8, thenounproject.com, CC BY-SA 2.0; **25** *cla*: (ic) Television by Adrien Coquet, thenounproject.com, CC BY-SA 2.0; **25** *clb*: (ic) Baby by Emily Keller, thenounproject.com, CC BY-SA 2.0; **26** *tl* & **27** *tr*: (ic) Wreath by Alex Muravev, thenounproject.com, CC BY-SA 2.0; **26** *clb*: (ic) Space by IronSV, thenounproject.com, CC BY-SA 2.0; **27** *cl* & **27** *clb*: (ic) poet by Phạm Thanh Lộc, thenounproject.com, CC BY-SA 2.0; **28** *tl* & **29** *tr*: (ic) Coins by Evgenii Likhachov, thenounproject.com, CC BY-SA 2.0; **28-42** *w*: (m)(ph) White Concrete Wall by rawpixel.com; **30** *tl*: (ic) Army by Viral faisalovers, thenounproject.com, CC BY-SA 2.0; **31** *tr*: (ic) Office by Anggara Putra, thenounproject.com, CC BY-SA 2.0; **32** *tl*: (ic) Tractor by Olivier Guin, thenounproject.com, CC BY-SA 2.0; **33** *tr*: (ic) School Desk by Jongrak, thenounproject.com, CC BY-SA 2.0; **34** *tl*: (ic) Exams by Arjan Farzkenari, thenounproject.com, CC BY-SA 2.0; **35** *tr*: (ic) Children by IronSV, thenounproject.com, CC BY-SA 2.0; **35** *clb*: (ic) sweets by Lars Meiertoberens, thenounproject.com, CC BY-SA 3.0; **36** *tl* & **37** *tr*: (ic) Home by Numero Uno, thenounproject.com, CC BY-SA 2.0; **38** *tl*: (ic) Roast chicken by Slurp Design, thenounproject.com, CC BY-SA 3.0; **39** *tr*: (ic) Fruit by novani, thenounproject.com, CC BY-SA 2.0; **40** *tl* & **41** *tr*: (ic) Fashion by Mahmure Alp, thenounproject.com, CC BY-SA 2.0; **42** *tl*: (ic) Holiday by Claudia Revalina, thenounproject.com, CC BY-SA 2.0; **43** *tr*: (ic) Christmas Tree by Azam Ishaq, thenounproject.com, CC BY-SA 2.0; **43** *w*: Christmas (m) © Annie Spratt, Unsplash.com; **44** *tl*: (ic) Entertainment by shashank singh, thenounproject.com, CC BY-SA 2.0; **45,47,49** *tr* & **46,48** *tl*: (ic) Clapper Board by Andrew Nielsen, thenounproject.com, CC BY-SA 2.0; **50** *tl*: (ic) Radio by GreenHill, thenounproject.com, CC BY-SA 2.0; **51,53** *tr* & **52** *tl* : (ic) Old TV by Eko Purnomo, thenounproject.com, CC BY-SA 2.0; **54,56** *tl* & **55** *tr*: (ic) Record by Mourad Mokrane, thenounproject.com, CC BY-SA 2.0; **57** *tr*: (ic) Music Note by Karen Tyler, thenounproject.com, CC BY-SA 2.0; **58** *tl* & **59** *tr*: (ic) Trumpet by Valter Bispo, thenounproject.com, CC BY-SA 2.0; **60** *tl*: (ic) Arts by Kelsey Armstrong, thenounproject.com, CC BY-SA 2.0; **61,63** *tr* & **62** *tl*: (ic) Book by Travis Avery, thenounproject.com, CC BY-SA 2.0; **64** *tl* & **65** *tr*: (ic) Theatre by Ben Davis, thenounproject.com, CC BY-SA 2.0; **66** *tl* : (ic) Sculpture by Creative Mania, thenounproject.com, CC BY-SA 2.0; **67** *tr*: (ic) Poetry by Martin, thenounproject.com, CC BY-SA 2.0; **68** *tl* & **69** *tr*: (ic) Airplane by Vectors Market, thenounproject.com, CC BY-SA 3.0; **68-73** *w*: (ph) Electricity (m) © Hal Greenwood, Unsplash.com; **70** *tl* & **71** *tr*: (ic) Microscope by Yoshi, thenounproject.com, CC BY-SA 3.0; **72** *tl*: (ic) Old Television by Eko Purnomo, thenounproject.com, CC BY-SA 3.0; **73** *tr*: (ic) Clapper Board by Andrew Nielsen, thenounproject.com, CC BY-SA 3.0; **74** *tl*: (ic) Mountain by Vectors Market, thenounproject.com, CC BY-SA 3.0; **74** *w*: (ph) Mountains (m) © Jordan Heath, Unsplash.com; **75** *tr*: (ic) DNA by Nawicon, thenounproject.com, CC BY-SA 3.0; **75** *w*: (ph) Double Helix (m) © Braňo, Unsplash.com; **76** *tl*: (ic) revolver by Kevin, thenounproject.com, CC BY-SA 3.0; **76** *w*: (ph) Prison Bars (m) © weston m, Unsplash.com; **77** *tr*: (ic) Cross medal by Juicy Fish, thenounproject.com, CC BY-SA 3.0; **77** *w*: (ph) Waves (m) © César Couto, Unsplash.com; **78** *tl*: (ic) Skull by Tina Rataj-Berard, thenounproject.com, CC BY-SA 3.0; **78** *w*: (ph) Skulls (m) © Malcolm Lightbody, Unsplash.com; **79** *tr*: (ic) Tornado by Aquariid, thenounproject.com, CC BY-SA 3.0; **79** *w*: (ph) Storm Clouds (m) © Nikolas Noonan, Unsplash.com; **80** *tl*: (ic) Earthquake by KonKapp, thenounproject.com, CC BY-SA 3.0; **80** *w*: (ph) Damaged Building (m) © Jose Antonio Gallego Vázquez, Unsplash.com; **81** *tr*: (ic) Flood by WiStudio, thenounproject.com, CC BY-SA 3.0; **81** *w*: Sea (m) © Matt Hardy, Unsplash.com; **82** *tl*: (ic) Football by leo-graph.com, thenounproject.com, CC BY-SA 2.0; **82** *w*: Football Pitch (m) © Alberto Frías, Unsplash.com; **83** *tr*: (ic) Tennis by Mister Pixel, thenounproject.com, CC BY-SA 2.0; **83** *w*: Tennis Court (m) © M. Z., Unsplash.com; **84** *tl*: (ic) Rugby Ball by Marco Livolsi, thenounproject.com, CC BY-SA 2.0; **84** *w*: Rugby Match (m) © Alex Motoc, Unsplash.com; **84** *h*: Rugby Lineout © Auckland Museum, Wikimedia Commons, CC BY-SA 4.0; **85** *tr*: (ic) Cricket by Bernd Lakenbrink, thenounproject.com, CC BY-SA 2.0; **85** *w*: Cricketer (m) © Yogendra Singh, Unsplash.com; **86** *tl*: (ic) Horse Racing by Sergio Morozov, thenounproject.com, CC BY-SA 2.0; **86** *w*: (ph) Racehorse (m) © Luisa Peter, Unsplash.com; **86** *h*: Horse Race © Jongsun Lee, Wikimedia Commons, CC BY-SA 3.0; **87** *tr*: (ic) Race Car by Slidicon, thenounproject.com, CC BY-SA 2.0; **87** *h*: Race Car © (ph) Jeff Cooper, Unsplash.com; **87** *w*: (ph) Chequered Flag (m) © Bas van den Eijkhof, Unsplash.com; **88** *tl*: (ic) Boxing Glove by Anton Anuchin, thenounproject.com, CC BY-SA 2.0; **88** *w*: Boxing Match (m) © Johann Walter Bantz, Unsplash.com; **89** *tr*: (ic) Golfer by Nicolas Vicent, thenounproject.com, CC BY-SA 2.0; **89** *w*: Golfing (m) © Courtney Cook, Unsplash.com; **89** *h*: Golf Ball (m) © mk. s, Unsplash.com; **90,92** *tl* & **91,93** *tl*: (ic) Framed Picture by Lil Squid, thenounproject.com, CC BY-SA 2.0; **94** *tl* & **95** *tr*: (ic) Camera by AomAm, thenounproject.com, CC BY-SA 2.0; **96** *tl*: (ic) Present by Vinzence Studio, thenounproject.com, CC BY-SA 2.0

Join our mailing list

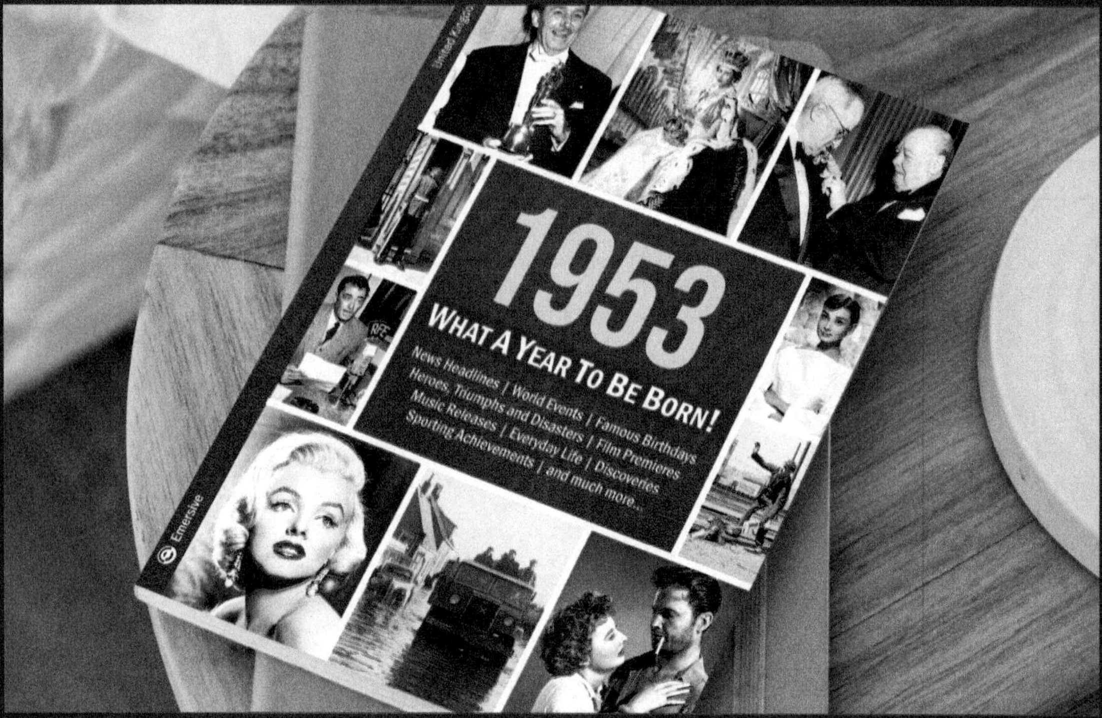

Join us for news on our future releases, reader promotions and behind-the-scenes content. All at:

www.subscribepage.com/whatayear

It's completely free to join. As a subscriber we will email you no more than once or twice a month. We will never share your email address and you can unsubscribe at any time.

Answers to the Eleven-plus Exam on page 34

Arithmetic Questions

Q1: The motorist has travelled 202 miles
Q2: 314
Q3: The ship could travel 120 miles
Q4: Four hundred and sixty five
Q5: A) Elizabeth's father was 36 years old
Q5: B) In 7 years' time
Q5: C) Elizabeth will be 30 years old

General Intelligence Questions

Q1: A) **Billy** was stung by **a** bee.
Q1: B) The shepherd **stood** by the gate and **whistled** to his dog.
Q1: C) The **family** went to the pool for a **swim**.
Q2: A) Coconut
Q2: B) Giraffe
Q2: C) Patricia
Q3: A) When the dog saw me, it wagged **its** tail.
Q3: B) The subject doesn't concern you or **me**.
Q3: C) Whilst speaking to my brother, the police car **passed** me.

Printed in Great Britain
by Amazon

29912140R00057